FROM LIMA TO LETICIA

The Peruvian Novels of Mario Vargas Llosa

Marvin A. Lewis

UNIVERSITY
PRESS OF
AMERICA

LANHAM • NEW YORK • LONDON

Copyright © 1983 by

University Press of America,™ Inc.

4720 Boston Way
Lanham, MD 20706

3 Henrietta Street
London WC2E 8 LU ENGLAND

Printed in the United States of America

Library of Congress Cataloging in Publication Data

Lewis, Marvin A.
   From Lima to Leticia.

   Bibliography: p.
   Includes index.
   1. Vargas Llosa, Mario, 1936-   --Criticism and
interpretation. I. Title.
PQ8498.32.A65Z712   1983   863   83-1057
ISBN 0-8191-3049-4
ISBN 0-8191-3050-8 (pbk.)

For Judy, Monica and Kevin--Latin Lovers

iv

ACKNOWLEDGEMENTS

I would like to thank the Research Board of the University of Illinois for their financial support and Leticia Díaz and Stephen Fleming for their help in preparing this manuscript.

TABLE OF CONTENTS

viii

PREFACE

With the awarding of the Nobel Prize to the Colombian writer, Gabriel García Márquez, Spanish American literature is once again the focus of international attention. At the forefront of this consistent excellence in literary creativity, alongside García Márquez, are writers of stature such as the Mexican, Carlos Fuentes, and the Peruvian, Mario Vargas Llosa, to name a few. These three exemplary intellectuals are related conceptually in that to better appreciate their works an understanding of sociology and history is just as important as an appreciation of narrative technique. García Márquez, Carlos Fuentes, and Vargas Llosa, to a degree, are all concerned with defining and interpreting Spanish American culture.

My interest in Vargas Llosa was initially stimulated by the late Professor Joseph Sommers, to whom I am greatly indebted. This early interest has been fueled over the years by my own investigations into Peruvian culture, the results being the present effort to elaborate upon some of the salient characteristics of the novels of Mario Vargas Llosa.

INTRODUCTION

MARIO VARGAS LLOSA: THE MAN AND HIS WORKS

Mario Vargas Llosa is today one of Peru's most talented and controversial men of letters. Although his reputation is based on the success of his novels, Vargas Llosa has written numerous scholarly articles and several books of literary criticism on both Peruvian and international topics. Vargas Llosa's major novels include: La ciudad y los perros, The Time of the Hero (1963), which deals with adolescent life in a military school; La casa verde, The Green House (1966), an examination of both rural and urban aspects of Peruvian existence; Conversación en La Catedral, Conversation in The Cathedral (1969), a work assessing a critical period in Peruvian history; Pantaleón y las visitadoras, Captain Pantoja and the Special Service (1973), a satire of the military, criticizing blind devotion to duty; La tía Julia y el escribidor, Aunt Julia and the Scriptwriter (1977), a semi-autobiography assessing the art of literary creation from a parodic perpective; and La guerra del fin del mundo, The War of the End of the World (1981), which interprets a Brazilian religious conflict. Five of these novels are interpretations of Peruvian reality.s.

Vargas Llosa also has to his credit a collection of short stories, Los jefes, The Chiefs (1959) and a short novel, Los cachorros, The Cubs (1967). In 1981 his play, La señorita de Tacna, The Lady from Tacna appeared. The author's earlier novels have been translated into more than a dozen languages, among them English, German, French, Russian, and Yiddish. At home and abroad his works have received critical scrutiny in the form of numerous articles, monographs and dissertations. As a reflection of the high acclaim afforded his novels throughout Europe and the Americas, Vargas Llosa has probably had more awards bestowed upon him than any novelist in Latin America.

In the area of literary criticism too, Vargas Llosa has been busy. Two of his most important publications are García Márquez: Historia de un deicidio, García Márquez: History of a Deicide (1971) and La orgía perpetua: Flaubert y Madame Bovary, The Never Ending Orgy: Flaubert and Madame Bovary (1975). In the first of these studies, which grew out of his doctoral thesis, Vargas Llosa applies his own theories concerning the writer as supplanter of God in the

creation of a fictional world to the works of
Colombia's leading novelist. The second study is an
analysis of the masterpiece by Flaubert, the writer
who Vargas Llosa credits with having had the greatest
impact upon his technique. In addition to the
international dimension of his criticism, Vargas Llosa
has dedicated many articles to Peruvian writers
and trends.

Life

Mario Vargas Llosa was born on March 28, 1936 in
Arequipa, Peru, in the home of his maternal grand-
parents. His parents had separated shortly before
his birth. At the age of one Mario and his mother
accompanied her parents to Cochabamba, Bolivia where
Vargas Losa's grandfather served as a government
employee. The family spent eight years (1937-1945) in
Bolivia where, by his own admission, Vargas Llosa led
a sheltered and pampered life. Mario and his mother
were united with her husband in Piura, Peru and they
remained there a year before moving to Lima.

During the brief stay in Piura Vargas Llosa had
begun his first attempts at creative writing. Upon
returning to Lima he spent short periods of time in
several schools and finally entered the Leoncio Prado
military academy, an experience that left an indelible
mark on his personality. The two years, 1950-52, in
this institutuion were designed to mold Vargas Llosa
into a man since his father was not pleased with the
youngster's previous soft upbringing. The environment
was a survival of the fittest situation designed to
prepare the cadets for their successful entry into the
real world. Students from all segments of Peruvian
society were brought together with their diverse values
intact. Vargas Llosa reacted negatively to the
socialization process and graphically described some
of its shortcomings in La ciudad y los perros. He did
not finish the program of study at the Leoncio Prado
but returned to Piura to complete this phase of his
education. In Piura Vargas Llosa enjoyed brief
artistic success with the staging in 1952 of his play
"La huida del Inca" which has since fallen into
literary oblivion.

The period following these educational experiences
was one of intensity. Vargas Llosa worked for news-
papers, radio stations, and on other odd jobs in order
to survive while keeping abreast of studies in

literature and law at the University of San Marcos in Lima. It was a time of demanding literary activity, maturation, and matrimony. His financial problems were compounded by the fact that at age 19 in 1955 he married his thirty year old Bolivian "aunt" Julia Urquidi, who was in reality the sister of a woman married to Vargas Llosa's uncle. The marriage lasted for nine years.

Nevertheless Vargas Llosa's literary and newspaper activities continued to increase. He completed most of the short stories which were to be collectively known as Los jefes and published in 1959. His efforts culminated in the winning of a trip to France in 1958, as a result of the short story competition organized by the magazine Revue Française. "El desafío," "The Challenge" was the prize winning entry. This story relates a duel to the death between two men for the sake of honor and machismo. In this selection the reader receives insight into the violent and bloody world which Vargas Llosa will develop in much of his later fiction.

The month long trip to Paris, which went with the award, stimulated more interest in Europe on Vargas Llosa's part. Later in 1958 he returned to Europe as recipient of the Javier Prado scholarship from Peru to study at the University of Madrid. This opportunity allowed Vargas Llosa to travel and to expand his literary and cultural activities. The following year his collection of short stories Los jefes won the Leopoldo Alas prize in Spain and signaled the beginning of a long and productive publication career for Vargas Llosa. The years 1959-1974 were spent in Europe working at various jobs, studying literary theory, teaching, and writing, except for brief trips to Peru to reacquaint himself with his culture. The distance between himself and the reality which he interpreted posed problems for Vargas Llosa since he was in danger of losing contact with the people and the environment which he portrayed in his works.

Nevertheless, he remained in Europe for several reasons. In addition to the stimulating cultural environment, more opportunities to publish were available. Secondly, the distance from Peru gave him a better perspective from which to write as well as an opportunity to discipline himself. Finally, the political and economic conditions in Peru were not favorable for a professional writer who believed that

Socialism was the best route for his country to follow. In spite of financial hardships endured initially in Paris, Vargas Llosa remained true to his convictions and thrived.

His persistence was rewarded in 1963 with the publication of La ciudad y los perros. Vargas Llosa received the Spanish Critics Prize for this effort which assured him of international fame. His reputation as one of Latin America's leading writers was solidified with the publication of La casa verde in 1966. For this outstanding novel Vargas Llosa also recieved the Critics Prize in Spain, the newly endowed Rómulo Gallegos in Venezuela, as well as the Peruvian National Novel Prize in 1967. As a leading novelist, critic, and outspoken advocate for freedom of the press, he was constantly invited to give conferences and courses in literature in England, Puerto Rico and the United States. In 1967, also, Vargas Llosa published the short novel Los cachorros, which has been made into a motion picture depicting adolescent insensitivity and brutality among Peru's middle class.

If Vargas Llosa's popularity as a writer reached its high point in Caracas with his "Literature is Fire" speech, his literary trajectory peaked with Conversación en La Catedral published in 1969. In this lecture he gave upon receiving the Rómulo Gallegos Prize, Vargas Llosa elaborated upon his ideas concerning the duties and the attitudes of commited Latin American writers.[1] He made two basic points which are related. First of all, the Latin American writer exists in a virtual cultural vacuum without the proper environment or stimulation necessary for artistic production. There are not enough people who are capable of reading or buying their books. The second idea advanced by Vargas Llosa is that writing literature means inconformity and rebellion and that the very being of the writer is bound up with protest, contradiction, and criticism. Literature, for him, is a permanent form of insurrection. To his credit, Vargas Llosa has been faithful to these convictions throughout his literary career.

Critics have lamented the fact that his latter novels have not reached the same level of critical realism present in Conversación en La Catedral. The concensus concerning Pantaleón y las visitadoras and La tía Julia y el escribidor is that they amplify his literary horizons but do not enrich the overall development of Vargas Llosa's novelistic output. Since his return from Barcelona, his residence since 1970, to Peru in 1974 Vargas Llosa has enjoyed continued fame and literary success as both critic and creative writer. As Peru's most well known literary figure he has access to the media and is constantly sought out for social and literary opinions. The controversial nature of Vargas Llosa's career was demonstrated during 1971 in his reaction surrounding aritistic freedom in Cuba. Initially he had supported the Cuban Revolution, but when pressure was placed on the Cuban poet Heberto Padilla to qualify some of his anti-revolutionary writings, Vargas Llosa disassociated himself from the cultural institution Casa de las Américas. He, in turn, was strongly criticized by Haydée Santamaría, the directoress, for being more interested in money than culture or revolutions.

In 1971 Vargas Llosa's doctoral dissertation, García Márquez: Historia de un deicidio appeared. It is a rigorous critical examination of this Colombian writer and the creative function. Another monograph, La orgía perpetua: Flaubert y Madame Bovary, published in 1975, is an analysis of the masterpiece by Flaubert, the writer who Vargas Llosa claims to be his primary literary model. These studies are valuable to the public because they provide insight into how Vargas Llosa views himself as a writer. He remarks in the latter study that Flaubert is the writer that he would like to have been. In the analysis of Madame Bovary, Vargas Llosa discusses the initial conception of the book by Flaubert as well as its internal and external structure. He dwells upon the themes of violence, melodrama, and sex. More importantly, Vargas Llosa views Madame Bovary as the first modern novel in terms of narrative technique.

In the study on García Márquez, Vargas Llosa applies some of the techniques used in his own works, but most importantly he defines the total novel, an achievement which has so far eluded him. According to Vargas Llosa the total novel describes a closed world from birth to death in all its aspects, "the individual and the collective, the legendary and the historical, the mundane and the mythic." The author as creator manipulates this world describing "an image of reality which is at the same time an expression and a negation of that reality." Cien años de soledad embodies all of these critical considerations from Vargas Llosa's point of view.

Since 1969 Vargas Llosa has published two Peruvian novels while remaining active on the world literary scene. _Pantaleón y las visitadoras_ (1973) recounts the process by which an army officer establishes a prostitution service for isolated military posts in the Iquitos region of Peru. The protagonist is so obsessed with perfecting the system that he destroys his own military career. The movie was banned in Peru. _La tía Julia y el escribidor_ (1977) has been criticized for not being as problematic as one would expect from Vargas Llosa. It is an autobiographical novel which alternates between the courtship and marriage of Mario and Julia in 1955 and the adventures of a writer of radio soap operas. This work presents the opposite side of Peruvian life from _Conversación en La Catedral_ which also transpires during Odría.

Living in Peru from 1974 to the present has not changed Vargas Llosa's style significantly since he continues to publish, give speeches and participate in Peruvian cultural and intellectual life. In Peru these activities have been curtailed somewhat by media censorship which he vehemently opposes. His outspoken defense of artistic freedom won for him the Godó Llallana Prize in Barcelona in May 1979. At home Vargas Llosa was recently ostracized by the military government because of his critical views of the ordering of priorities in Peru. In July of 1979 he, along with other Chilean and Peruvian intellectuals, came under attack because of their plea for better understanding between the two countries one hundred years after the War of the Pacific in which Chile decisively defeated Peru and Bolivia. In his defense of their unpopular position Vargas Llosa pointed out that Peru's problems are within the country itself and not in Chile.

Upon stepping down as President of the Pen Club he announced _La guerra del fin del mundo_, a novel dealing with an episode of Brazilian religious history which represents a radical change from his previous literary perspective. Vargas Llosa still resides in Lima with his second wife, Patricia, and their children.

The Peruvian Context

Vargas Llosa's prose fiction is a mirror of his times. It is particularly an interpretation of problems inherent in the society of Peru, a developing Latin American country. As a realist writer, Vargas

Llosa expresses concerns regarding militarism, the
power of the oligarchy and the adverse situation of
the masses. Most of the attendant symptoms of
underdevelopment, such as social inequities, injustice,
exploitation, and discrimination, are woven into the
fabric of his major novels. Vargas Llosa's early
works, La ciudad y los perros and La casa verde are
situated in the years 1931-1963. Historically this
was a period of political, social, and economic
instability which is characterized by the many forms
of government from the military rule of Luis Sánchez
Cerro to civilian control under Manuel Prado.

During this era many phenomena occurred which
changed the fabric of the Peruvian nation.[2] They
include a rapid population growth in the cities,
industrialization, increased life expectancy, electri-
fication of the country, and the emergence of strong
political parties. The most important of these
organizations and their leaders were APRA, American
Popular Revolutionary Alliance (Victor Raúl Haya de la
Torre); Socialist (Hildebrando Castro Pozo); and
Communist (José Carlos Mariátegui). 1948-1956 was of
prime importance because it marked the military
dictatorship of Manuel Odría who was accused of leading
one of the most corrupt and repressive regimes in
modern Peruvian history. Odría's eight year reign
is further characterized by heavy United States
investment and financial domination of the country.

The period 1963-1975 is also influential in the
development of Mario Vargas Llosa's literary career.
Politically the poles are Fernando Belaúnde Terry and
General Juan Velasco Alvarado. In 1975 Velasco was
replaced by General Francisco Morales Bermúdez, who
remained in power until the return to civilian rule
in May 1980 with Belaúnde again at the helm. The
military government of Velasco Alvarado, 1968-1975, is
singled out as one of progress and reform. Major
achievements by this administration were in the
following areas: 1) agrarian reform, including land
expropriation and a push for more respect for the
indigenous peoples; 2) nationalization, of petroleum,
mining, communications, railroads, airlines, fishing,
and banking; and 3) depoliticalization, or decreasing
the influence of the leading political parties. Under
Velasco also, the power of the oligarchy was broken.

Vargas Llosa expressed cautious optimism about
these changes although he was not overly pleased with

the military character of the Revolution and the lack of popular participation. He was enthused, however, by progress in the agrarian and petroleum sectors; in the international politics, and in the industrial community. Changes in the structure of the country made Peru a more inviting place for Vargas Llosa to return to, which he did in 1974.

In spite of the progress achieved in returning Peru to the Peruvians, the Velasco Alvarado government faced serious problems of cash flow and inflation as a result of the importation of food and other necessities, as well as the adverse impact of natural disasters such as floods and earthquakes on the country. Also due to media criticism a strict censorship was imposed in 1974 which remained in effect through 1980. The military government had taken over the media from its owners and replaced top level officials with government appointees. Vargas Llosa's reaction to censorship at the time was critical as he maintained that the credibility of the Revolution had suffered irreparable damage. On numerous occasions he has reiterated his views, most recently as he relinquished the Pen Club presidency and declared that, "the fight against shameful censorship is, for the writer, more than an ethical question: it is a necessity of cultural survival and its non existence is essential in order for intellectual work to be creative." Vargas Llosa goes on to say that each time a writer is exiled, or prohibited from leaving the country or when a book is confiscated, all intellectuals are being threatened.

The succession of many styles of government over the past decades with varying degrees of success reiterates the fact that Peru is a difficult country to govern because of a number of environmental, political, biological, and cultural factors. These constraints and their impact on the human condition are the subject matter of the literature of Mario Vargas Llosa.

Vargas Llosa's literary production is an interpretation of Peruvian reality. The inner workings of society, specifically the military, the class structure, the process of urbanization, and the political system, are all within the realm of his literary scope. Vargas Llosa has considered himself a committed writer whose duty it is to point out societal inequities. He views the artist, through

writings and actions, as an active participant in the
solution of the economic, political and social problems
of a given country.

Vargas Llosa reaffirmed these beliefs at the
Oklahoma Conference dedicated to him in 1977 in a
speech titled, "Social Commitment and the Latin
American Writer." He sets forth the writer's position
by stating, ". . . that the political commitment of
writers and literature in Latin America is a result
not only of the social abuse and economic exploitation
of large sectors of the population by small minorities
and brutal military dictatorships. There are also
cultural reasons for this commitment, exigencies that
the writer himself sees grow and take root in his
conscience during and because of his artistic development. To be a writer, to discover this vocation and
to choose to practice it pushes one inevitably, in our
countries, to discover all the handicaps and miseries
of underdevlopment."

Therefore, in his major novels, from La ciudad
y los perros through Pantaleón y las visitadoras,
Vargas Llosa has been concerned with criticizing
Peruvian institutions. In La ciudad y los perros the
military school, Leoncio Prado, is presented as a
microcosm of society. Its primary responsibility is
to instill into the cadets values prevalent in the
larger society. Hence lying, cheating, and even murder
are condoned insofar as they facilitate the
socialization process and assure the individual of
advancement.

La casa verde is concerned with the geographical
impact of the country upon its inhabitants. The
immense Amazonian jungle is juxtaposed to the Piuran
desert and both serve as natural backdrops for human
failure. The limited possibilities of heroism because
of environmental and cultural constraints is one of
the novels's basic thrusts.

Conversación en La Catedral is a political novel
which reflects the corruption of an era. Domination
of the individual and of the country is complete due
to the repressive forces of a military dictatorship.
The four hour "conversation" is carried on by two
opposite individual perspectives, an alienated
bourgeois intellectual and a poverty stricken black,
both portrayed as victims of societal forces. Thus
the question "¿En qué momento se había jodido el Perú?"

is a motif which prefigures a close examination of many aspects of Peru during the military dictatorship of General Manuel Odría.

Militarism is the focus in Pantaleón y las visitadoras which offers an in-depth look at army functions from an ironical perspective. Blind devotion to a cause is the apparent narrative focus but the novel is actually a criticism of the Center of Higher Military Studies which was created in 1950. The purpose of this center was to stimulate officers to solve long standing social problems. In his own way, this is precisely what Pantaleón did by turning his prostitute service into the most efficient arm of the military.

La tía Julia y el escribidor is less problematic in nature in terms of addressing itself to the larger questions of society. However, it is in part auto-biographical and does reflect many middle class Peruvian values and attitudes prevalent during the Odría era. This novel interprets a segment of the same period as Conversación en La Catedral but emphasis is placed upon the author's love life and his perceptions of the person who wrote radio novels. The sentimental, the improbable, as well as the Peruvian presence in the autobiographical segments make the novel good reading.

In the majority of his novels Vargas Llosa employs the latest technical innovations of the new Latin American Narrative, such as flashbacks, interior monologs, fragmented time sequences and breaks in the narrative structure. Maximum reader participation is required in order to piece together incidents often separated temporally and spatially. Many times there is an attempt to recreate the thought patterns of a protagonist. Vargas Llosa's attitude is that in order to capture the complex realities that he attempts to convey, a complicated technique is appropriate. Verbal, situational, and metaphysical irony is employed as a key ingredient in the literary strategy. The clash between expectation and realization heightens the dramatic impact in all of his fictional works. Many intercalated episodes are often present within a larger framework.

Mario Vargas Llosa has enjoyed phenomenal success both at home and abroad. Outside of Peru this is due to the fact that he is an extraordinarily talented writer who is at the forefront of the "Boom" in Latin American literature. In Peru Vargas Llosa's achievements as a novelist can be attributed to his ability to solve the relationship between the needs of his audience and the artistic presentation of those needs. His most successful novels in Peru are those which treat the Peruvian middle class and their environment. The public, it seems, is more comfortable when it reads literature reflecting its own experiences. For instance La tía Julia y el escribidor has been very popular because the middle class reader can identify cultural points of contact associated with the Peruvian milieu which are not overtly critical of Peru. On the other hand, La ciudad y los perros was denounced for being scandalous when it first appeared.

Vargas Llosa is consistently the best of the Latin American novelists who have gained world wide recognition in recent years during the so-called Boom. Others, such as the Mexican writer, Juan Rulfo, or the Colombian, Gabriel García Márquez, have written a better single novel than Vargas Llosa. But none of this group can match his output in terms of both consistency and creativity. Through a combination of form and content Vargas Llosa has succeeded in creating a body of work that appeals to a wide audience. By limiting himself to the Peruvian ethos he has not constructed a cultural barrier, but rather Vargas Llosa has facilitated the reader's interpretation of what he attempts to portray.

Method

The present study analyzes four major novels of Mario Vargas Llosa: La ciudad y los perros (1963), La casa verde (1966), Conversación en La Catedral (1969), and Pantaleón y las visitadoras (1973). My focus is upon works interpreting Peruvian reality. The purpose of this book is to shed light on various techniques and themes of these novels in order to show how they contribute to Vargas Llosa's overall view of the human condition in Peru. Following basically a thematic approach, elements examined include the ironic mode and its relationship to the novelistic structure; the notion of the hero; philosophical underpinnings such as determinism and existentialism; and the author's view of the process of Peruvian history.

This analysis seeks to reveal that the study of the central thematic matrix of the novels and the special literary shadings in its presentation can lead to the definition of a set of meanings and an interpretation of reality. The critical approaches followed in the study, therefore, are a combination of the culturalist and the formalist. Both an intrinsic and an extrinsic examination of the novels are undertaken. The author's style and technique are studied insofar as they relate to the vision of reality portrayed in the novels. Vargas Llosa demonstrated artistic complexity more clearly, perhaps, than any other Latin American novelist. As a new novelist he is inextricably bound up with social and historical concerns and philosophical questioning.

Chapter organization is designed to include elements which will aid in a progression toward a tentative interpretation of Vargas Llosa's attitudes toward Peruvian society, in particular, and the human condition in Latin America in general. Chapter one explores the concept of heroism and its implication within the context of the works examined. Different ramifications of the heroic ideal are manifested in the author's literary production, varying from traditional to new interpretations.

Chapter two is concerned with the importance of irony in the narrative structure of Vargas Llosa's works. In addition to situational and verbal irony, the author's portrayal of characters and circumstances entails a peculiar manner of presenting the clash between expectation and realization. Extended to the metaphysical level, this clash presents man contemplating an indifferent universe in his efforts to make life meaningful.

Chapter three discusses the philosophical theories of determinism and existentialism and their importance in the author's world view. The opposition between the two doctrines, which has been singled out by critics, is discussed in an effort to show how the author weaves these two forces coherently into his literary projection.

Chapter four, lastly, deals with the author's assessment of Peruvian history. Different periods are explored, such as the epochs of Sánchez Cerro and Odría. The manner in which the author chooses to interpret historical material is studied. Also, the treatment of the Indian, the presence of APRA, and the class conflict are examined in the light of their presentation in the novels.

The conclusion analyzes, briefly, the parodic dimension of La tía Julia y el escribidor and its relationship to the earlier novels of Vargas Llosa. A general summary rounds out this study.

NOTES

[1] The text is contained in the document "El Premio Rómulo Gallegos," Mundo Nuevo, No. 17 (Nov. 1967), pp. 92-95.

[2] This discussion is based upon ideas contained in Henry F. Dobyns and Paul L. Doughty, Perú: A Cultural History (New York: Oxford University Press, 1976), pp. 224-66.

CHAPTER 1

HEROISM: A FRAGILE STATE

The novels of Mario Vargas Llosa embody various literary conceptions of the hero. One encounters fledgling adolescents, military men, popular-mythic individuals, as well as the anti-hero. In this examination of the theme of heroism in Vargas Llosa's novels, characters discussed will include Alberto, Jaguar, and Gamboa of La ciudad y los perros; Anselmo and Fushía of La casa verde; Santiago of Conversación en La Catedral; and Pantaleón of Pantaleón y las visitadoras.

Some of the standard definitions of the term "hero" are outdated for modern literary purposes. The modern protagonist no longer manifests traditional heroic virtues. In most definitions of the word, "hero" becomes synonymous with protagonist or leading character with whom the audience sympathizes and who is the focal point of interest in the activity. The hero is the individual who normally reflects the author's system of values as set forth in the work of fiction. If the author is creating a work which encompasses a positive outlook on life, usually the hero will exemplify such characteristics as astuteness, courage, and fortitude.

However, since the heroic is a dynamic concept it usually operates in direct relationship with the system of values of a given society. In the contemporary cultural context, traditional heroic qualities are not viewed in the same light as they were in antiquity. Rather, the concept exemplified by Vargas Llosa and his contemporaries is that of the introspective or existential hero who is neither more nor less than an ordinary person in his fight for survival. His battles are of a personal, symbolic nature rather than an overt manifestation of prowess.

For decades artists have written with the conviction that the age-old ideal of heroism being synonymous with monumental achievements was outmoded in bourgeois society. The "unheroic" individuals who evolved as fictional protagonists helped to define a new concept of heroism by being complex, sensitive individuals who usually present serious problems concerning the human condition often without the

1

necessary means for solving them. Irving Howe contends:

> The modern hero moves from the heroic
> deed to the heroism of consciousness,
> a heroism often available only in
> defeat. . . . And in consciousness
> he seeks those moral ends which the
> hero is traditionally said to have
> found through the deed.[1]

This contemporary existential view of the hero portrays
existence in the Sartrean vein as an ongoing crisis of
consciousness. The existential hero is faced with the
problem of self definition and with seeking justification for his position in the universe. He is often
torn between the desire to act and the belief that
action is absurd since the dilemma of exercising his
options is constantly before him. The modern existential hero is faced with the problem of survival in a
spiritual sense. In existential terms his principal
quality is that of becoming, as his struggle is toward
"being." This leads to an introspective presentation
of protagonists and circumstances in literature.

As the traditional hero became more ordinary, the
idea of the anti-hero evolved, and the anti-hero is
looked upon today as one of the standard examples of
a fictional protagonist. The concept of the anti-hero
as a reflection of the changing norms of heroism has
been traced to the late eighteenth century. However,
Fyodor Dostoyevsky's Notes from Underground (1864)
is often singled out as the work which marked somewhat
of a turning point in the evolution of the anti-hero.[2]
Just as the hero expresses acceptable values of a
society, the anti-hero will embody, for the most part,
values considered negative by society which are
reflected in the context of the work.

The critical assumption expressed here is that
there are basically two types of anti-heroes. First
of all, there is the "achiever" who fails. This
character is in the macho mode and has the capacity
to be heroic by taking risks, is brave, and has the
power to command. But his values soon lead to moral
or social disparity. Secondly, there is the character
who tries but cannot succeed, in the schlemiel manner.
Whereas the former type embodies negative social values,
the latter is likely to receive a certain amount of
reader sentiment. As Nadia Christensen points out

in her evaluation of the anti-hero, "He proves unequal to the challenge he is faced with, he gains no reward, and he is never fully reconciled to the ordinary world."[3]

Hero and anti-hero, then, are therefore closely related and not identified as the complete antithesis of each other. Northrop Frye sums up, convincingly, the situation of both hero and anti-hero in his "Theory of Modes" when he states: "If inferior in power or intelligence to ourselves so that we have the sense of looking down on a scene of bondage, frustration, or absurdity, the hero belongs to the ironic mode."[4] According to Frye, ironic literature with the frustrated hero or anti-hero is characteristic of most fiction of this century. This, in turn, is related to techniques employed in the New Novel, such as the new view of time and the presentation of the nature of consciousness.

In most instances time is viewed as durée, or duration, a Bergsonian concept in which we do not separate the past from the present or from the future. All states merge into one, as time is not set up in any order. The mental processes of individuals are dealt with in this fluctuating time dimension and the reader engages in the struggles of protagonists. Often a life time is captured within days or hours as witnessed in the agonizing deathbed experiences of, for example, Artemio Cruz or in the revolutionary transcity trip of Andrés in País portátil. These are but two anti-heroes who exemplify the temporal dimension of the Latin American novel in the search for identity and authenticity in life.

In sum, contemporary heroism becomes more 'existential'--an internal phenomenon rather than an outward manifestation of actions. The hero has been stripped of most of his traditional mythic qualities and therefore seeks new definitions along with personal justification for his actions and existence. He usually looks to self rather than to others for approval of his actions.

Vargas Llosa's main characters are presented in a manner comparable to most modern literary protagonists. The reader encounters in his fictional world ordinary protagonists who are often difficult to understand, incapable of outstanding actions, trapped by the

3

circumstances, banal, and in disagreement with themselves. Viewed in their Latin American context, Vargas Llosa's heroes, along with those of José Donoso and Carlos Fuentes, have been labeled "degraded" by Luis B. Eyzaguirre. The contemporary generation of heroes, he maintains, has much in common, including their fictional presentation: "Sin ilusiones que sustentar, los fracasos de los personajes no son tanto eso como miradas retrospectivas a la cadena de circumstancias que los ha puesto en la situación en que ahora se encuentran."[5]

Their common denominator is the inability to excel as a result of societal and personal constraints which limit individual achievement. This is not to say that transitory successes are not accomplished; on the contrary, many insignificant individual battles are won but Vargas Llosa's protagonists do not overcome the important obstacles. The question this chapter addresses is how, at given moments, these individuals display modern heroic virtues such as selflessness, capacity for sacrifice, risk, solidarity, and rebellion. The crucial issue, from a critical perspective, is how Vargas Llosa's literary protagonists imbued with universal heroic traits, respond to Peruvian cultural limitations.

LA CIUDAD Y LOS PERROS

In La ciudad y los perros character studies of two adolescents, Alberto and Jaguar, and a mature member of the Military Establishment, Lieutenant Gamboa, will suggest the nature of this heroic potential in Vargas Llosa's literary protagonists. Alberto and Jaguar obviously have not fully developed their systems of values. But during the novelistic sequence of La ciudad y los perros it is possible to see how each goes about attempting to define himself in a heroic manner. They are shown to combine both old and new ideas in their process of self destruction.

Since the adolescents are in a state of "becoming" and unable to perform great deeds, heroism involves relating to one another on a personal level within the closed environment of the Leoncio Prado. This entails a certain amount of selflessness, which involves solidarity with the group and the willingness to sacrifice oneself. The acts and attitudes, of course, are not without guilt-provoking moments.

4

Alberto and Jaguar are very different in social and psychological makeup. Alberto's experience is more of a traditional middle class one. It comes to us narrated more or less in a straightforward manner with few flashbacks and interior monologs. Vital information concerning the identity of Jaguar is withheld, however, engrossing the reader on a deeper level in the complexity of his fight for survival. Narrative technique is very important in our perception of the characters. Multiple points of view, broken chronology and interior monolog allow the reader to approach the protagonists through their interior and exterior lives. This is revealing in terms of their motivations. Plot structure, too, with focus on the suspenseful, helps to highlight individual acts.

During the early stages of La ciudad y los perros one of the boys is very tender in his relations with a girl, Tere. But he is also capable of violence as shown in the episode where he attacks another youth who goes to the beach with Tere. Later we see the same character robbing houses with Flaco Higueras. The witholding of the character's identity affects our overall perception of him, since we are not able to equate him with Jaguar of the Leoncio Prado who he ultimately turns out to be. As presented, this early character has a certain heroic aura about him as demonstrated in his willingness to battle difficult odds to achieve his goals.

Whereas Alberto knows how to manipulate people and situations, Jaguar is respected for his ferocity and adherence to a strict honor code which has become vital to him through the years. A single incident in the novel, the death of Ricardo Arana, brings to the fore the best that these two have to offer in terms of heroism.

El Jaguar apparently kills Ricardo, "el Esclavo," who has betrayed Cava, a member of the Círculo, the Club, over which Jaguar presides. Believing that the worst crime imaginable is to be a soplón, or squealer, Jaguar takes it upon himself to carry out the beliefs of his honor code. Alberto, who is supposed to be a friend of Arana, tells Lieutenant Gamboa of all the cadets' clandestine activities as he accuses Jaguar of murder. Gamboa intends to take action against Jaguar after having him confined. The efforts of Alberto and Jaguar land them both in jail for a final confrontation:

　　　　--No grites imbécil, van a oírte.
No lo maté. Cuando salga, buscaré
al soplón y delante de todos le haré
confesar que es una calumnia. Vas a
ver que todo es mentira.
　　　　--No es mentira--dijo Alberto--.
Yo sé.
　　　　--No grites, maldita sea.
　　　　--Eres un asesino.
　　　　--Chist.
　　　　--Yo te denuncié, Jaguar. Yo sé
que tú lo mataste.
　　　　Esta vez Alberto no se movió. El
Jaguar se había encogido en la tarima.
　　　　--¿Tú le has dicho a Gamboa?--dijo
el Jaguar muy despacio.
　　　　--Sí. Le dije todo lo que has
hecho, todo lo que pasa en la cuadra.
　　　　--¿Por qué has hecho eso?
　　　　--Porque me dio la gana.
　　　　--Vamos a ver si eres tan hombre--
dijo el Jaguar incorporándose.6

　　Emphasis in this scene is on Alberto's self
affirmation as he seeks, for the first time, to prove
to Jaguar that he is not afraid of him. Throughout
the novel Alberto has avoided harassment and punishment
by being able to dissimulate and avoid placing himself
in tense situations. In this confrontation with Jaguar
all pretenses are put aside and it becomes a question
of hombría, or masculinity, for both of them. Alberto
fights a courageous battle but his reward proves to be
a severe beating at the hands of Jaguar and the promise
of expulsion from the school if he does not keep quiet
about Ricardo's death. The authorities will not
tolerate a scandal.

　　Alberto, known as "the Poet," is presented in the
novel as being distinct from most of the other cadets.
He has a creative bent and uses this talent to help
himself survive by writing letters for the others and
by exercising the pornographic aspects of his imagination. His thoughts are usually of a poetic nature
and his literary aptitude keeps him aloof from the
rest of the boys. As a result he is rather bored and
seeks to outwit most of his companions with his mental
games. Earlier, signs of rebellion in Alberto, against
school and the established order, had been noted by
his father, who sent him to the Leoncio Prado for

6

discipline. But Alberto, as most of the cadets, feels
the need to be an individual.

Alberto's sole heroic act in the novel is thwarted
both physically and mentally. Gamboa tells him:

> . . . usted no puede acusar a nadie,
> no puede ser juez de nadie. Si yo
> fuera director del colegio, ya estaría
> en la calle. Y espero que en el futuro
> suprima ese negocio de los papeluchos
> pornográficos si quiere terminar el
> año en paz. (p. 305)

Alberto receives a physical and verbal lashing. Gamboa,
who has obviously been swayed by the colonel, is also
reacting against the thought of being outwitted by
the cadets. Alberto, motivated in part because of
guilt, does not receive much satisfaction from the
Ricardo Arana affair. After this moral high point, he
proceeds to go downhill.

Alberto is willing to risk himself to transcend
his defensive realistic posture. The system uses his
other transaction in order to blunt the thrust. It
can tolerate an anti-hero, but not a full blown
crusading hero.

Given his particular situation Alberto realizes
that it is useless to fight against the system now
that all the odds are against him. Thus in the end
he is forced to drop his heroic posture and acquiesce
to his true middle class values. Alberto is restricted
by a built-in social code of behavior which forbids
him to endanger reputation, family, and class. He
helps to perpetuate the system, just as his father
hoped he would. Alberto allows his heroic flame to
flicker briefly and die.

Jaguar acts according to his convictions probably
more convincingly than any other character in the novel.
It is he who tries to set an example of toughness for
the cadets with the formation of the Círculo and his
teachings of self preservation. Jaguar is the model
whom the others want to emulate because of his early
resistance to punishment and his fight for self
respect as a perro, or first year cadet.

The fact that Jaguar has strong beliefs makes it
more difficult for him to be broken after his is
accused by Arróspide of betraying his entire section.
Alberto is really the culprit:

> "¿Qué espera?" pensaba Alberto. Hacía unos
> momentos, bajo la venda, había brotado un
> dolor que abarcaba ahora todo su rostro.
> Pero él lo sentía apenas; estaba subyugado y
> aguardaba, impaciente, que la boca del Jaguar
> se abriera y lanzara su nombre a la cuadra,
> como un desperdicio que se echa a los perros,
> y que todos se volvieran hacia él asombrados
> y coléricos. Pero el Jaguar decía ahora,
> irónico:
> > --¿Quién más está con ese miraflorino?
> No sean cobardes, maldita sea, quiero saber
> quién más está contra mí. (p. 310)

Alberto expects Jaguar to tell what he knows but this
would be a breach of his code. Refusing to be a
soplón, Jaguar remains defiant to the end. The cadet's
opinion of him has changed but what matters to Jaguar
is that he remains loyal to himself. He maintains
his consistent posture even though he suffers a severe
beating at the hands of the cadets. Ostracized by
his mates and no longer looked upon as their leader,
el Jaguar struggles to retain personal consciousness
and risk of self.

Both cadets react to the Arana incident in a way
which they believe to be justified. Alberto's
reaction is more external because he has always managed to face life on a superficial level. He is willing to take certain risks but knows when to stop. On
the other hand, heroism is implied by Jaguar's conception of life, both externally and internally. He is
willing to risk imprisonment in order to protect his
moral beliefs. Reluctantly, he realizes at the end
that all of the outward masculinity which he has
tried to teach the cadets is worthless. Until they
try to face reality, as he does under pressure, they
will not be able to overcome their immediate circumstances and assert themselves as individuals.

Even Ricardo Arana, the catalyst, who does not
offer much in terms of overt heroism, has his personal internal moments of triumph. As he is about to
play the role of squealer he reflects upon his unhappy
days in the Colegio Salesiano. Tired of being everybody's whipping post, he reacts:

> Una vez se dijo: "tengo que hacer algo." En
> plena clase desafió al más valiente del año:
> ha olvidado su nombre y su cara, sus puños cer-
> teros y su resuello. Cuando estuvo frente a
> él, en el canchón de los desperdicios, encerra-
> do dentro de un círculo de espectadores ansi-
> osos tampoco sintió miedo, ni siquiera excita-
> ción: sólo un abatimiento total. (p. 119)

In his mind Ricardo makes the association of this
heroic act with the final defiant one of betrayal as
he lies dying in the infirmary. Certainly for him
they are important events in his short life. In the
early development of characters in La ciudad y los
perros, internal heroism is accentuated by our knowledge, via a variety of techniques, of the internal
processes of characters' minds. This is quite apparent
in our perception of thoughts in the early development
of Alberto, Jaguar, and Ricardo.

Each of the cadets discussed displays various
forms of heroism whether the act involves the risk
of extending help to another as in the case of Alberto,
adherence to a moral code as exemplified by Jaguar,
or exposing oneself to ridicule as Ricardo does. The
acts are consistent with the types of characters portrayed.

Gamboa, more than any other soldier in La ciudad
y los perros shows the ability to think and act inde-
pendently. As Gamboa prepares the shakedown inspec-
tion and charges against Jaguar, Captain Garrido warns
Gamboa of the consequences. Although future promotions and a military career are at stake Gamboa re-
plies:

> --A mí me interesa el ascenso tanto como a
> usted, mi capitán. Haré todo lo posible por
> conseguir ese galón. Yo no quería ser des-
> tacado aquí, ¿sabe usted? Entre esos mucha-
> chos no me siento del todo en el Ejército.
> Pero si hay algo que he aprendido en la Es-
> cuela Militar, es la importancia de la disci-
> plina. Sin ella, todo se corrompe, se malo-
> gra. Nuestro país está como está porque no
> hay disciplina, ni orden. Lo único que se
> mantiene fuerte y sano, es el Ejército, gra-
> cias a su estructura, a su organización. Si es
> verdad que a ese muchacho lo mataron, si es
> verdad lo de los licores, la venta de exámenes

y todo lo demás, yo me siento responsable, mi
capitán. Creo que es mi obligación descubrir
lo que hay de cierto en toda esa historia.
(p. 262)

Gamboa, as his simple direct language indicates,
is acting because of beliefs which are very personal
to him. He feels that the cadet's actions not only
threaten the school but are symptomatic of the makeup
of Peru in general. His obligation is to do justice
regardless of the obstacles involved, despite the
fact that his military future could change drastically.
Gamboa's conscientious devotion to duty is a part of
his understanding of what being a military man is all
about. After a momentary vacillation he decides to
continue the investigation. He knowingly embarks on
a campaign to change the status quo but his end is
predictable.

However, Gamboa too has the personal satisfaction
of knowing that he follows his convictions to the
bitter end. As Captain Garrido tries to smooth over
his exile to Puno, Gamboa tells him: "--No me gusta
que me compadezcan, mi capitán. Yo no me hice militar para tener la vida fácil. La guarnición de Julia-
ca o el Colegio Militar me da lo mismo" (p. 322).
For Gamboa the military, being a heroic profession,
embodies certain risks which he is willing to take.
Gamboa's heroism like Jaguar's, assumes more significance because it is not allowed to be completely
snuffed out.

Here, too, a certain amount of irony is involved.
The theory which Gamboa so strongly holds to is in
conflict with practice. The violators of the military code get the promotions and the assignments
while the defenders' fate is semi-exile.

As long as he does perform his duty which includes
a considerable amount of self satisfaction and expression of beliefs, Gamboa as an individual is able to
satisfy certain personal goals. Individual heroism,
however, is not favored by society at large since the
system is based upon conformity. And in the end,
Alberto, Jaguar and Gamboa do conform to the higher
demands of society and the military. Jaguar adapts
more or less on his own terms while Alberto's and
Gamboa's attempts at asserting themselves are obstruc-
ted by the military. They all have heroic moments but
even within the closed world of the Leoncio Prado, the

10

the heroic process is shown to be one leading
to frustration.

LA CASA VERDE

This pattern continues and becomes even more
pronounced in La casa verde which deals with mature
people in difficult circumstances, who also lead a
structured life. La casa verde is basically concerned
with various fights, for survival which demand that
the characters constantly be prepared to put forth
their best efforts. Anselmo and Fushía, as hero and
anti-hero respectively, represent outstanding
variations of the heroic mode.

An example of an active hero who is impeded in
his efforts to excel is Anselmo of La casa verde.
Anselmo begins heroically in the archetypal concept
of the word. Commenting on "Initiation" as a variation
of the Hero Archetype, Wilfred F. Guerin and his
co-editors explain: "The Hero undergoes a series of
excruciating ordeals in passing from immaturity to
social and spiritual adulthood, that is, in achieving
maturity and becoming a full fledged member of his
social group."7 This study is primarily concerned
with Anselmo's "achieving maturity and becoming a
full fledged member of his social group," which involves
a process of self realization and acceptance by others
during his period of Initiation. Anselmo's projections
as archetypal hero has been discussed by Michael Moody
in his dissertation.

The function of Anselmo and his relationship to
the Green House grow to mythic proportions in the
popular mentality of the Mangachería. Anselmo, along
with Domitila Yara and Sánchez Cerro provide residents
of this barrio with a much needed sense of pride and
self-esteem. The need for myths and heroes is indeed
great for these oppressed people since this barrio
is a prime example of Peruvian internal colonialism.

The living conditions of the Mangachería demand a
form of mental escape which manifests itself in
remembrances of an imaginative individual (Anselmo),
a popular saint (Domitila), and an ex-president
(Sánchez Cerro). But the images of heroism projected
are negative as reflected in the actions and the
final life stories of Sánchez Cerro and Anselmo. Both
end in frustration and death.

11

In the traditional sense, mythification is recognized as the last stage in the development of a hero. During the novelistic process of La casa verde, Vargas Llosa successfully employs techniques to aid the heroic/myth making procedure. There is a difficulty created in zeroing in on Anselmo and the Green House because of the shifting points of view, broken chronology in the time sequence, and doubts in the minds of characters themselves as we are presented brief moments of consciousness. Whether or not the Green House existed becomes secondary to the characters as each one adopts versions which suit his personal needs. What is important is the personal triumph of Anselmo:

> Y un día los piuranos admitieron que
> don Anselmo vencería, al divisar al
> otro lado del río, frente a la ciudad,
> como un emisario de ella en el umbral
> del desierto, un sólido, invicto
> esqueleto de madera. A partir de
> entonces, el trabajo fue rápido.[8]

Don Anselmo apparently has won the initial battle with nature, but the more difficult one with human nature is yet to be waged. The Green House becomes a popular house of prostitution which immediately draws the wrath of Padre García, moral guardian of the community. Tragedy strikes for Anselmo when the blind and mute Antonia, his mistress, dies giving birth to La Chunga. An enraged mob inspired by García promptly burns the Green House to the ground.

Over a period of years the inhabitants begin to question whether indeed it had really existed:

> Se ha hablado tanto en Piura sobre la
> primitiva Casa Verde, esa vivienda ma-
> triz, que ya nadie sabe con exactitud
> cómo era realmente, ni los auténticos
> pormenores de su historia. Los super-
> vivientes de la época, muy pocos, se
> embrollan y contradicen, han acabado
> por confundir lo que vieron y oyeron
> con sus propios embustes. Y los
> intérpretes están ya decrépitos, y es
> tan obstinado su mutismo que de nada
> serviría interrogarlos. En todo caso
> la originaria Casa Verde ya no existe.
> (p. 97)

This confusion of fact with folklore is essential in heroic myth making. The vivienda matriz, a type of archetypal abode, gives origin to a set of popular beliefs which are essential to the mangache spirit.

Anselmo's rise and fall are inseparable from the Green House. His success in defying the established order, i.e., the sands representing nature, and society, in the form of Padre García, remains alive for the people even though decades have passed since the occurrence of the events. This success, due to courage, perseverance and capacity for sacrifice, elevates him to the stature of hero even though he ends up defeated. Ironically, only in defeat can Anselmo become a real mangache, acceptable to the community and with whom the popular elements can identify. Gone is the knight on the black trick horse and in his place remains Anselmo, a member of the pueblo.

After Anselmo's defiant temporary triumph over the established order, although he is of unknown origin, he gradually becomes one of the mangaches because the Mangachería is made up almost entirely of people who have suffered greatly from their day to day experiences in life. Mangache life is constructed around defeatist images of experience which vary from the physical setting itself to the portrayal of its heroes, including Sánchez Cerro, whose image popular mythology carefully shapes, along with that of Anselmo. Life in the Mangachería does not project many positive images. Anselmo temporarily provides this need:

> En la fantasía popular, el pasado de
> don Anselmo se enriquecía, a diario
> se añadían a su vida hechos sublimes
> o sangrientos. Viejos mangaches
> aseguraban identificar en él a un
> adolescente que años atrás perpetró
> atracos en el barrrio y otros afirma-
> ban: "es un presidiario desertor, un
> antiguo montonero, un político en
> desgracia." Sólo el Padre García se
> atrevía a decir: "su cuerpo huele
> a azufre." (p. 103)

The projection of Anselmo as hero combines both traditional and mythological elements with the idea of the modern hero. Early in life he is the person

who "slays the dragon" and later he is nothing more
than the disconcerted, alienated harp player in the
second Green House. Padre García links Anselmo with
biblical mythology, the Devil, and Sodom and Gomorrah.
Along the way Anselmo undergoes a tremendous fall
which, ironically, immortalizes him in the popular
imagination.

The final destinies of Anselmo and the Green
House are similar. Collectively their fates are
inseparable and after a brief defeat Anselmo and the
Green House both return, but in different forms. For
a while the order of things is disturbed, only to be
resumed amidst memories and rumors of what might have
been. However, Anselmo is resurrected as the harp
player in the band of el joven Alejandro and el Bolas
as la Chunga begins to restructure the lifestyle in
the Mangachería with the building of the second
Green House.

Anselmo's approach to the entire affair,
understandably, remains ambiguous. He denies that the
institution ever existed, probably because of the
memory of his personal tragedy with Antonia. On the
other hand he takes a great deal of pride in being
involved in the rebirth of the system which he started
and which is now being propagated by his daughter. In
this respect his initial dream lives on as he shares
in the experience which he had begun years earlier.
Anselmo has accepted a more conventional role in
society and lives the rest of his days as harpist,
although for the people of the Mangachería he remains
a true hero.

In his definition of the modern-psychological
novel Victor Brombert offers a critical observation
which is applicable to Anselmo:

> His inner moral standards, and even
> more, his awareness of his elusive
> "self," depends on the vision of the
> "others," on the combination of
> acceptance and rejection of their
> judgment. Hence the growing importance
> of images of guilt, prisons and
> trials. On the other hand, his quest
> for identity inevitably leads to the
> age-old question of meaning, salvation,
> redemption and survival in a spiritual
> sense.[9]

Anselmo as a literary hero goes through the process
of acceptance and rejection as he is always aware of
what image he is projecting. One of his greatest
desires it to be accepted by the mangaches. He never
absolves himself of the guilt he feels for the death
of Antonia, hence the retreat into his personal world
of darkness. His momentary indulgence in alcoholism
and self degeneration exemplify this attitude.

Images of guilt, prisons and trials normally
shape the structure of Vargas Llosa's novels and
the destinies of major characters, including Anselmo.
Protagonists of his novels are plagued by these
phenomena. Inhibited in the outer world, they all
seek refuge in inner thoughts and desires, groping
for new insights and values to existence. Their
search for meaning, salvation, and moral redemption
becomes more of a personal challenge. Heroism, most
of them discover, is truly an act of self assertion
of morality.

Exemplifying one aspect of the anti-heroic mode
in Vargas Llosa's works is the figure of Fushía who
incorporates some of the negative connotations
associated with the anti-hero. Carlos Fuentes labels
him, "Fushía, bastardo, ladrón y contrabandista."[10]
However, studied in the complexity of his presentation
in La casa verde, Fushía as anti-hero embodies both
good and evil and is far from being a one dimensional
figure.

Fushía appears early in the narrative as he and
Aquilino have embarked on a trip to the leper colony
of San Pablo. The voyage is twofold, for Aquilino will
not only serve as guide on the river but will also
function as pseudo-psychiatrist while he and the reader
probe Fushía's troubled mind. Thus Fushía's life is
presented in retrospect with a juxtaposition of dialogs
and monologs. Time has been suspended as significant
events are brought into focus without regard for their
chronological occurrence. In this descent into the
"underworld" of his mind, Fushía seeks answers to vital
questions concerning his existence.

Being a great lover had been one of Fushía's
illusions, but he failed miserably. Thoughts of Lalita,
his concubine, constantly haunt him: "Me acuerdo de
esa puta todo el tiempo--dijo Fushía--. Es tu culpa,
Aquilino, hace dos noches que me la paso viéndola y

15

oyéndola. Pero como era de muchacha, cuando la conocí" (p. 70). Fushía keeps living the romantic past in which he performed in a heroic manner, first wooing and then eloping with Lalita, his princess, and taking her away from the evil opposition of Julio Reátegui. On his island, however, Fushía's dreams were to be shattered as Lalita proceeded to lose her beauty and his virility faded. Instead of the macho he pictured himself as being, Fushía became a household joke for all the women on the island. In his present anti-heroic situation he can only resort to memories of the past.

In her assessment of the anti-hero Christensen writes: "A unique blend of ingredients from tried and true recipes, he incorporates significant characteristics of his direct ancestors--the heroes of classic epic, of romance and of tragedy."[11] The parallels break down rather quickly however. Fushía as anti-hero only superficially incorporates some of these characteristics. Whereas the traditional hero was gifted with the capacity to perform exceptional deeds, Fushía is not. For example, when directing raiding parties he stays in the background and when he actively participates, he becomes nauseated at the sight of atrocities commited. Fushía is not a personal warrior by any stretch of the imagination. On the other hand, his feat in setting himself up as a sort of conquering lord has epic proportions.

Fushía does show similarity to the tragic hero in his function as a type of scapegoat in La casa verde. His predicament is tragic in the sense that he moves from a touch of glory to misery and suffers more than the average. Although Fushía considers himself a sacrificial victim, he is not atoning for anybody's sins but his own. This also lends a note of tragedy to the situation.

As anti-hero he is portrayed as not being completely innocent or guilty. Fushía is, rather, a victim of 'arbitrariness;' the reader gets the impression that things could possibly have turned out differently at Campo Grande and that Fushía is not totally responsible for his plight. This point is raised in a significant discussion with Aquilino:

> --Pero entonces no eras malo--dijo
> Aquilino--. Tú mismo me dijiste que
> eras honrado.

16

<pre>   --Antes de entrar a la cárcel--
        dijo Fushía--Ahí dejé de serlo. (p. 31)</pre>

Prison, one of the constant images in Vargas
Llosa's works, once again serves to shape a character's
destiny. It was in prison that Fushía was exposed to
ruthlessness and was able to see man's inhumanity to
man. As a result, he lost many human qualities such
as honesty and credibility. Due to early factors, a
great deal of Fushía's life is filled with suffering.
His anti-heroic world never becomes a rational or
orderly place. This is reflected in the agonizing
nature of the voyage which leads to his ignoble death:
"--Una playita, viejo--dijo Fushía--Por nuestra
amistad, Aquilino. No a San Pablo, déjame donde sea.
No quiero morirme ahí, viejo" (p. 344). Traditionally,
the hero's death had an air of nobility about it, as
death was welcomed or encountered while fighting for a
cause. Fushía, anti-hero, is alone, afraid, and
desperately trying to avoid his end as he erodes both
physically and spiritually. Encapsulated within the
month-long time dimension, Fushía's experience is one
of dying rather than deeds.

The traditional hero moved customarily on an
upward plane. Our view of Fushía begins as a horizontal
one but quickly takes a downward plunge to correspond
with his trajectory. The final vision which the reader
receives is that of looking down on a scene of complete
frustration as Fushía awaits death at the leper colony.
For him, important events have truly "salido al revés,"
as he maintained earlier. Fushía's aspirations and his
accomplishments are very much out of proportion. He
wins a few skirmishes but always manages to lose the
big battles. Money, which he fought so ruthlessly to
obtain, is wothless to him in the end. As shown in
La casa verde, Fushía, anti-hero, undertakes the
archetypal quest--not for personal glory, but for
meaning. The result of this quest is a lack of
comprehension of the complexities of human existence.

CONVERSACION EN LA CATEDRAL

Santiago Zavala, in Conversación en La Catedral,
embodies a different kind of heroic ideal than most
of the others presented by Vargas Llosa in his novels.
He is best described as the disillusioned Sartrean type
bourgeois intellectual. Constatly at war with his
environment, he finds that the existing political
reality has made survival impossible for him. Thus,

17

as Victor Brombert notes:

> An intellectual hero thus came into
> being, often politically committed,
> also in revolt against his bourgeois
> background, flirting with the myths
> of revolution, tragically torn between
> militant desires and a chronic sense
> of guilt.[12]

Zavalita is searching basically for pattern and
destination in his life. As an existential hero
Santiago's acts lack conclusive meaning, for they are
carried out in the process of "becoming." He goes into
self-imposed exile because he does not approve of his
father's relations with the Odría regime. After his
unsuccessful revolutionary days in San Marcos and his
failure as a member of the Communist cell Cahuide,
Santiago sinks into cynicism and despair. His political
commitment is questionable as he only "flirts with the
myths of revolution," never putting himself in a truly
vulnerable situation. When the moment arrives, he
refuses to join the Communist Party.

Santiago tries desperately to lose his class
identity by marrying Ana, a lower class person, and
carrying out a bohemian existence. This fails, however,
because he always remains loyal to his family even
though he does not share in their prosperity. The
entire social process which Santiago observes from a
distance instills within him a sense of guilt toward
self, country, and fellow man. As he asks the question:
"¿En qué momento se había jodido el Perú?,"[13] Santiago
seeks justification for both his own failure and that
of his country.

In the four-hour conversation with Ambrosio,
Santiago's entire experience consists of a restructur-
ing of his past, trying to determine where he went
wrong. His married life has been filled with mental
anguish since Ana never forgave him for not accepting
his inheritance:

> Si no se lo hubieras contado a Ana
> te habrías ahorrado muchas peleas,
> piensa. Cien, Zavalita, docientas.
> ¿Te había jodido la vanidad? piensa.
> Piensa: mira qué orgulloso es tu marido
> amor, les rechazó todo amor, los mandó

18

al carajo con sus acciones y sus casas
amor. ¿Creías que te iba a admirar,
Zavalita, querías que? Te lo iba a
sacar en cara, piensa, te lo iba a repro-
char cada vez que se acabara el sueldo
antes de fin de mes, cada vez que
hubiera que fiarse del chino o prestarse
plata de la alemana. Pobre Anita,
piensa. Piensa: pobre Zavalita.
(II, p. 297)

Santiago considers the fact that he disinherited
himself a heroic act. This is reflected in "mira
que orgulloso es tu marido amor, les rechazó todo
amor, los mandó al carajo con sus acciones y sus casas
amor." The reality of the situation, however, has
been brought out in material terms. The contradiction
of overt pride and inner guilt relfected in the above
passage reveals the ambiguous attitude which Santiago
feels toward his circumstances: "¿Creías que te iba
a admirar, Zavalita, querías que?"

The use of an accusative voice of conscience in
this instance enables Zavala to recapture many moments
of turmoil which he has experienced as a result of his
decision to withdraw from the bourgeois world.
Repetition of the verb pensar amplifies the amount of
mental anguish to which he is being subjected.

Santiago's quest for identity entails a questioning of meaning and existence, as he has chosen to seek
survival in a spiritual sense rather than become a
part of the system. His uncompromising posture,
refusing to compromise with bourgeois values, wife
and family, is consistent to the end, thus accentuating
his personal individual integrity which we see in his
internal processes. But this is achieved at the
expense of his material loss, and of a self induced
defeat as far as integration of the self is concerned.

PANTALEON Y LAS VISITADORAS

One of the extremes of the heroic ideal is
presented by Vargas Llosa in Pantaleón y las visitadoras. This novel concerns itself with the rise and fall
of Pantaleón Pantoja, an army captain who is sent to
Iquitos in the northern sector of Peru to provide a
service of visitadoras (prostitutes) for the troops in
that region. The basic problem which sets the novel

19

in motion is the fact that "la tropa de la selva se
anda tirando a las cholas."[14] The troops are commiting
sexual crimes against the women and the resulting turmoil keeps the jungle communities in an uproar.

Pantaleón's job is to provide an outlet for the
soldiers' sexual frustrations, which seem to be increased by the jungle environment. Known for his efficiency and ability to get the job done, he turns his
secret operation into one of the most efficient functions of the entire army. However, blinded by his success and dedication, Pantaleón loses his wife, Pochita,
and finally his position. He refuses to cooperate
with el Sinchi, radio commentator, when he demands a
bribe to remain silent about Pantaleón's activities.
This refusal leads to his being exposed by el Sinchi
and Maclovia, a prostitute.

But the biggest blow is dealt to Pantaleón when la
Brasileña, his mistress, is murdered and Pantaleón, considering his prostitutes an official part of the army,
eulogizes her while in uniform and gives her a full military funeral. The military establishment does not tolerate these actions, and therefore relieves Pantaleón
of his duties and posts him in Puno, the cold region,
near Lake Titicaca.

Humor, one of the elements absent to a large extent in Vargas Llosa's earlier novels, is one of the
basic ingredients in Pantaleón y las visitadoras. Humor, in this case, is intimately connected with the
theme of the absurd in the work. One also finds many
components of the comic novel in Pantaleón y las visitadoras; indeed, the propaganda jacket calls it "una
farsa y un apólogo". Pantaleón as a character is presented as a comic anti-hero who creates a system from
which he cannot liberate himself. He is not a mere
caricature, although there is a certain amount of sarcasm involved in his presentation.

Like the tragic anti-hero, the comic anti-hero
suffers and the reader does not identify with him out
of admiration because of the negative values which he
embodies. In contrast with the traditional comic hero,
the comic anti-hero's suffering is not temporary, nor
is it educational, nor does it compel him to conform
with the law through repentance or prudence. Rather,
the comic anti-hero is unable to rectify his mistakes
because of staunch beliefs in an ideal. In the case
of Pantaleón, it is the belief in discipline, in orders,

in hierarchy, in the military, in the system.

It is no coincidence that Pantaleón is an army
captain, considering the author's disdain for the
military. In a significant interview with Oiga
concerning the genesis of the novel Vargas Llosa
describes the character whom he has created:

> Siempre me fascinó este capitán o mayor
> seguramente de intendencia, que desde que
> salió de la escuela militar se debió
> ocupar de los ranchos de las prendas
> de vestir, del funcionamiento de los
> cuarteles, y que un buen día es llamado
> por sus superiores y se le encarga
> el organizar un servicio de prostitu-
> ción. Además discretamente sin que se
> entere la ciudadanía y seguramente
> su propia familia. A mí me pareció
> que el drama del personaje era real-
> mente muy estimulante.[15]

As the long quote continues Vargas Llosa reveals
the obvious enthusiasm with which he approached the
story of Pantaleón. His attitude borders on the gleeful
as he develops in a satirical manner, another of his
military characters. Pantaleón's entire presentation
in the novel is filled with irony as Vargas Llosa takes
a near perfect character and loses him in a sequence
of absurd actions. Pantaleón's activities and the manner
in which he goes about achieving his goals are highly
questionable. His self styled heroism compromises the
very institutions which he is trying to protect as he
shows a desire to make the visitadoras the most outstanding arm of the army.

The primary contradiction here is that the officers
who are in charge of more important duties such as
training and discipline are not as committed as Pantaleón. Even though his obligations are considered
secondary by some, Pantaleón's military mind makes it
necessary that he devote all of his energies to solving
the problem at hand. In Pantaleón y las visitadoras
Vargas Llosa offers a comic parodic view of military
procedure which is evident in the distortion of official
documents, procedures, communiques, and other related
command activities. The entire novel, as the title
suggests, is constructed around Pantaleón. The reader
observes most of his interpersonal relationships from

a distance and the manner in which he goes about his work is spectacular. There are four crucial relation- ships in the novelistic life of Pantaleón. They are with his wife Pochita, Padre Beltrán, la Brasileña, and the military itself. In each of these relationships Pantaleón fails to exercise discretion, a failure which is characteristic of the comic anti-hero.

Pantaleón's relationship with Pochita becomes strained as soon as he enters his secret service with the army. His recruitment of prostitutes entails long hours of night work which causes violent reactions:

> --Has estado con mujeres--estalla en
> sollozos Pochita--. Los hombres no se
> emborrachan hasta el amanecer sin mujeres.
> Estoy segura que estuviste Panta.
> --Pocha, Pochita, se me parte la
> cabeza, me duele la espalda--sujeta un
> paño sobre la frente, manotea bajo la
> cama, acerca una bacinica, escupe saliva
> y bilis Pantita--No llores, me haces
> sentirme un criminal y no lo soy, te
> juro que no lo soy. (p. 35)

Pantaleón's adaptation to his new role is rather pathetic at times. Variations of the above scene are repeated throughout the novel as he seeks to keep his activities a secret. What he succeeeds in doing is diverting information from himself only to have Pochita find out about his activities through her friends.

Padre Beltrán is opposed to the visitadora service because he believes in the spiritual gratification of man over the sexual. He does not appreciate the popularity of the movement, as he points out in his letter of resignation to General Roger Scavino which assails the success of the prostitute service.

Unwittingly, Pantaleón is starting a chain reaction of adverse events on all sides. Everything that he does produces an undesired effect, as he seems oblivious to the problems his pet project is creating. Padre Beltrán raises the moral/religious questions set forth in the novel by pointing out the obvious paradox in the priorities of the military which considers religion secondary to sex.

One factor which Pantaleón is unable to compensate for militarily is the attachment he feels for la

Brasileña. His predilection for her over the other
women leads to his becoming overly demanding and quite
jealous, as shown in one of several confrontations:

> --Ay, Panta, qué pesado eres--reniega,
> taconea, corre la cortina suspira mi-
> rando al techo, avienta su ropa al suelo
> con furia la Brasileña--. ¿No ves que
> estoy cansada, que acabo de trabajar?
> Y después ya sé lo que vendrá, la gran
> escena de celos. (p. 227)

Verbal accumulation helps to underscore and synthesize
the explicit tension in the scene as Pantaleón naively
imposes himself upon la Brasileña. Pantaleón's
approach to his affair with her is characterized by
a lack of tact which is a continuation of his method
of handling things in general. The author presents
him and his sexual exploits in a rather derisive
manner. Pantaleón's approach to his affair with her
is characterized by a lack of tact which is a continuation of his method of handling things in general.
The author presents him and his sexual exploits in a
rather derisive manner. Pantaleón's relationships
with women are shown as being boringly childish. He
is not a lover, as his actions and reactions reveal.
La Brasileña tolerates him because of the added priv-
ileges and money she receives as compensation.

Pantaleón considers himself an outstanding soldier
and therefore goes about his business in a professional
manner. The army, from the beginning, underestimates
his potential and is quite upset with the success which
he achieves, as suggested by General Scavino:

> Qué tragedia ni tragedia. El hijito de
> esa señora que va a llorarle, tiene gran
> parte de culpa en lo que ocurre. Si al
> menos hubiera organizado la cosa de una
> manera mediocre, defectuosa. Pero ese
> idiota ha convertido el Servicio de
> Visitadoras en el organismo más efi-
> ciente de las Fuerzas Armadas. (p. 225)

The "tragedia ni tragedia" reflects another aspect
of the paradoxical situation Pantaleón has created.
The army, known for its inefficiency, has suddenly
found success but in the wrong department. Encouraged
by his prosperity, Pantaleón can only think, logically,
of expanding the enterprise, even going so far as to

suggest hazardous duty pay for the visitadoras.
Pantaleón is so successful because he functions in a
way which everybody considers ridiculous. There is
a contradiction between his manner of viewing things
and what is considered the normal way. His heroic
valor is exercised on absurd projects which lead to
constant mishaps.

Pantaleón solves General Scavino's problem of
dismissal for him after the crucifixion of la Brasileña
by civilian bandits who wish to enjoy the visitadora
service themselves. The author uses newspaper cover-
age to report how Pantaleón reacts to her death in a
public eulogy:

> Hemos vestido nuestro glorioso uniforme
> de oficial del Ejército del Perú, para
> venir a acompañarte a éste que será tu
> último domicilio terrestre, porque era
> nuestra obligación proclamar ante los
> ojos del mundo, con la frente alta y
> pleno sentido de nuestra responsabilidad,
> que habías caído como un valeroso sol-
> dado al servicio de tu Patria, nuestro
> amado Perú. (pp. 252-53)

Pantaleón's speech is the last straw as far as the
army is concerned. Before, everybody knew or sus-
pected who he was and what he was doing and only com-
plained. Now that Pantaleón has publicly revealed
his function something has to be done--hence the
resulting exile. There is a clash between the reality
of the situation and its representation in the funeral
of la Brasileña. She is given a heroic funeral but
in an anti-heroic manner.

Pantaleón's success had been based upon the fact
that he did not comprehend fully the situation he was
in, rather than on heroic qualities such as courage,
fortitude, or unselfishness. But one does see a
great deal of human nature in Pantaleón as we contemplate his experience in a comic manner. There is a
fusing of the tragic sentiment with the comic narrative which is compatible with the comic spirit in
which the novel is written. B. N. Schilling asserts:

> If the comic experience is humane, cal-
> ling forth a sense of the richness of
> life, willing participation in it, an
> acceptance of the full responsibility

24

of being human, it also invites a certain discernment, an ability to see man as incongruously different from what he should be--a creature helpless before the needs of his body, weak, vain, and foolish when he might be greater in every way.[16]

Pantaleón y las visitadoras is a work filled with irony, humor, incongruencies and aberrations of human behavior. In this work Vargas Llosa treats humorously two of his major literary preoccupations, sex and the military, while bringing into focus aspects of the reality of Peru's jungle regions.

But regardless of the light tone employed in character and situational presentation, human degradation and exploitation, in the flesh traffic, and the absurdity of human actions, in the case of Pantaleón, are shown to be no laughing matter. Pantaleón as anti-hero places in critical perspective certain aspects of the military position in Peru.

Gamboa of _La ciudad y los perros_ and Pantaleón are two outstanding examples of how Vargas Llosa interprets the Peruvian military mentality. In spite of these officers' motivations and achievements, they are bound to fail. The author's satirical attack goes beyond mere invective and is not directed so much toward individual soldiers as it is toward the military complex.

In _Pantaleón y las visitadoras_ specifically, beneath the surface, the soldier per se is not the object of ridicule, but instead, the system that produced him. In the case of Peru it is the Centro de Altos Estudios Militares (CAEM) established in 1950. As Henry Dobyns and Paul Doughty point out,

> ...CAEM's short course format militated against full presentations of the complexity of issues and may well have tended to make solutions appear to officer students sheltered by their institution easier than in fact they were. In its first decade of existence, CAEM stimulated officers to solve long festering social problems.[17]

This is precisely what Pantaleón did. As a product of CAEM, he is incapable of reconciling his goals and the manner of achieving them. By embodying positive qualities such as courage, capacity for leadership and self sacrifice, and utilizing them to obtain negative ends, immorality and the dehumanizing aspects of prostitution, Pantaleón raises such issues as blind adherence to a code and inefficiency in administration. These are problems which the author views as fundamental in the relationship of military to country.

Throughout his novels, Vargas Llosa's characters painfully accept the fact that they are no more than ordinary, which is in conformity with the growing concept of heroism in the literature of this century. They are Peruvian, however, in the sense that they struggle within clearly defined cultural parameters such as the Leoncio Prado, the Amazonian jungle, the era of Odría, and the military bureaucracy. Applied to Vargas Llosa's literary creations these definitions ring remarkably true. The protagonists examined reveal a consistent pattern of rebellion and attempted self-assertion, however, followed inevitably by one form or another of defeat. Nevertheless, a number of personal and moral victories are recorded, for man's humanity is not denied. As exemplified in the number of protagonists thwarted despite their capacities for being heroic and who are forced to look inward to self for justification, Peruvian society does not subscribe to the overt excelling of man. At least in Vargas Llosa's particular interpretation of the situation, the structure of society and its institutions defines its own standards and the role which each individual has to carry out in his life.

As a result, Vargas Llosa's fictional representation of Peru appears unable to support a positive hero because of socially prevailing adverse values and the fact that humans are made of both positive and negative characteristics. His characters show a lot of potential but seldom realize their goals because of individual and societal limitations.

NOTES

[1] Irving howe, Decline of the New (New York: Harcourt, Brace & World, 1963), p. 30.

[2] Nadia Margaret Christensen, "A Comparative Study of the Anti-Hero in Danish and American Fiction" (Doctoral dissertation, Universtiy of Washington, 1972), p. 6.

[3] Christensen, p. 25.

[4] Northrop Frye, Anatomy of Criticism (Princeton, N. J.: Princeton University Press, 1957), p. 34.

[5] Luis B. Eyzaguirre, El héroe en la novela hispanoamericana del siglo XX (Santiago de Chile: Universitaria, 1973), p. 262.

[6] Mario Vargas Llosa, La ciudad y los perros (7th ed.; Barcelona: Seix Barral, 1962), p. 293. Cited hereafter in text.

[7] Wilfred F. Guerin, ed., A Handbook of Critical Approaches to Literature (New York: Harper & Row, 1966), p. 121.

[8] Mario Vargas Llosa, La casa verde (11th ed.; Barcelona: Seix Barral, 1966), p. 96. Cited hereafter in text.

[9] Victor Brombert, ed., The Hero in Literature (New York: Fawcett, 1969), p. 14.

[10] Carlos Fuentes, La nueva novela hispanoamericana (México: Joaquín Mortiz, 1972), p. 44.

[11] Christensen, p. 24.

[12] Brombert, p. 20.

[13] Mario Vargas Llosa, Conversación en La Catedral, 2 vols., I (5th ed.; Barcelona: Seix Barral, 19711), p. 13. Hereafter cited in text.

14 Mario Vargas Llosa, Pantaleón y las visitadoras (Barcelona: Seix Barral, 1973), p. 14. Cited hereafter in text.

15 "Vargas y su maldita pasión," Oiga Año 11, No. 487 (11 de agosto de 1972), p. 31. The image of Pantaleón now seems to be clearer than the vague notion expressed to Ricardo Cano Gaviria in 1971 in El buitre y el ave fénix (Barcelona: Anagrama, 1972), pp. 89-95.

16 Bernard N. Schilling, The Comic Spirit (Detroit: Wayne State Press, 1965), p. 17.

17 Henry Dobyns and Paul Doughty, Peru: A Cultural History (New York: Oxford University Press, 1976), p. 242.

CHAPTER 2

IRONY: THE DECEPTIVE MODE

Before exploring the ironic elements in Vargas
Llosa it is convenient, first of all, to examine some
of the different ramifications of this concept in
literature. Irony has various meanings and implications
which have changed over the centuries, but the basic
Greek interpretation of the word ("eironcia = dissimu-
lation"), remains at the root of its present day significance. Irony in a general sense involves both
verbal and situational expressions of a paradox or
incongruity; a contradicition usually forms the
basis of meaning.

Modern scholars distinguish between three basic
types of irony: verbal; dramatic; and metaphysical.
In The Encyclopedia of Poetry and Poetics one finds
the following explanation:

> Verbal irony is a form of speech in which
> one meaning is stated and a different,
> usually antithetical, meaning is intended.
> . . . Dramatic irony is a plot device
> according to which (a) the spectators
> know more than the protagonist; (b) the
> characters react in a way contrary to that
> which is appropriate or wise; (c) characters
> or situations are compared or contrasted
> for ironic effects, such as parody;
> (d) there is a marked contrast between
> what the play demonstrates about them.[1]

Metaphysical or cosmic irony is an extension of dramatic
irony in that it too is directly concerned with the
protagonist and his reaction to his circumstances.
Charles Glicksberg, in elaborating the added significance of irony for modern many, writes:

> Irony in its own right has expanded
> from a minute verbal phenomenon to a
> philosophy, a way of facing the cosmos.
> This metaphysical irony reveals a
> consistently disenchanting vision of
> the universe and man's place in it.[2]

Irony, then, is closely related to the human
condition and the artist's manner of contemplating it.
Irony is as much a feeling about the universe as a

stylistic technique. As set forth in Northrop Frye's
"Theory of Modes," in which modern literature is
classified as basically ironic, it is clear that the
modern artist expresses a very pessimistic view of
the human condition. This is precisely the attitude
of Vargas Llosa in his novels. Whether they are set
in Lima or the jungle regions, there does not seem
to be much hope for his characters who are either
overcome by the elements or by their fellow men.

The underlying conceptual basis of irony is
paradox, or the contrast between what is evident
and what is intended, either stated or implied. There
is a contradiction between the standards to which we
think a character or situation should conform and
what the author actually portrays. Since one of the
essential elements of irony is the reader's sense
of the clash between appearance and reality--in
characterization, novelistic structure, scenes or
language--, there must be a close collaboration between
author and reader in the recognition of different
levels of awareness, contradictions, and points of view.

The fact that three of Vargas Llosa's novels,
La ciudad y los perros, La casa verde, and Pantaleón
y las visitadoras, contain epilogs, and that Conversación en La Catedral is presented in retrospect, helps
to highlight the ironic results of individual acts.
In La ciudad y los perros it is the accused murderer
who adjusts most readily to society. La casa verde's
ending reveals a resolution of differences between good
and evil for the sake of the community. The circular-
ity of the protagonist's trajectory in Pantaleón y las
visitadoras highlights a lack of progress despite a
great deal of effort. The fact that two social outcasts are chosen to assess a period of Peruvian
history in Conversación en La Catedral lends an ironic
tone to the narrative perspective. The reader not only
witnesses the outcome of a particular set of
circumstances but also the manner in which they unfold.
This approach, often ironic, is in keeping with the
author's attempt to capture the totality of an
experience. For Vargas Llosa irony becomes a method
for examining the contradictory situations encountered
in the Peruvian experience.

Although critics have commented on the general
absence of humor in Vargas Llosa, the ironic
characteristics of his fiction have not been elucidated.

Verbal, dramatic, and metaphysical/cosmic irony and variations thereof are used throughout the four works under discussion. Vargas Llosa's way of contemplating the human condition and the forces which govern the interactions between characters in his novels is based on his ironic vision of the contradiction in human, and especially Peruvian, experience. This vision is set forth through style, subject matter, structure, characterization, tone, and unique manner of focusing on situations and events.

This chapter will examine pertinent ironic aspects of each major novel separately and then assess the importance of irony in Vargas Llosa's fictional world. Since it is virtually impossible to comment on all of the ironic possibilities, only a representative number of situations will be treated.

LA CIUDAD Y LOS PERROS

In most of his novels Vargas Llosa uses dramatic irony to enhance suspense and complicate overall structure. This technique is related to the development of character, plot, and scene. In La ciudad y los perros, for example, he has been criticized for using this device in the Teresa affair.[3] Teresa, at various points in the novel, is the girlfriend of Ricardo, Alberto and Jaguar, whom she finally marries. The development of these relationships is made more intriguing by their mode of presentation which involves the withholding of information concerning character identification.

Alberto takes advantage of Ricardo's naiveté when he is trusted to deliver a message for the latter. Ricardo never realizes that Alberto betrays his friendship and claims Teresa for his own. He is presented in the novel as being a helpless victim of an ironic situation, the complexity of which he does not grasp. Alberto is aware of Ricardo's plight as he and Teresa head for the movies:

> Decidieron ir al cine Metro. Alberto
> compró dos plateas. "Si Arana supiera
> para lo que ha servido la plata que me
> prestó, pensaba. Ya no podré ir donde
> la Pies Dorados." Sonrió a Teresa y
> ella también le sonrió."[4]

Ricardo never suspects that Alberto is betraying

31

him, although he raises the important question of
Alberto's loyalty without being aware of its true
implications. Alberto's success is lying to both
Teresa and Ricardo causes him to refuse to compose love
notes for the latter. Ricardo is clearly no match for
the wit and guile of Alberto. As presented throughout
La ciudad y los perros, Ricardo is the victim of the
other cadets, both overtly and, in this case, without
knowledge of the fact that he is being victimized.
Ricardo consistently receives the punishment of his
peers and finally makes the supreme sacrifice for all
of their guilts. Ricardo, who has been constantly
urged to act in a positive manner, is killed when he
finally asserts himself.

Jaguar is the exact opposite of Arana, both in
manner of presentation and characterization. We discover at the end of the novel that Vargas Llosa has
developed the character in such a way as to show a
complete change of personality. This evolution is
shown through the tender childhood love affair in
which Jaguar steals for Teresa; the brutal Jaguar
within the Leoncio Prado; and the finished product;
Jaguar married and a bank employee. The suspenseful
mode of presentation underscores the dramatic ironic
basis of the quadrangular affair.

The rediscovery of Teresa by Jaguar is told to
Flaco Higueras in the epilog as the former explains
his reactions after not having seen her for six years
and three months. Jaguar is overwhelmed by his good
fortune:

> --¿Y tú qué hiciste" --dijo el Flaco
> Higueras.
> --Le dije otra vez: "hola, Teresa. ¿No
> te acuerdas de mí?"
> Y entonces ella dijo:
> --Claro que sí. No te había reconocido.
> El respiró. Teresa le sonreía, le
> tendía la mano. El contacto fue muy
> breve, apenas sintió el roce de los dedos
> de la muchacha, pero todo su cuerpo se
> serenó y desaparecieron el malestar, la
> agitación de sus miembros, y el miedo.
> --¡Qué suspenso! --dijo el Flaco
> Higueras. (p. 337)

The utilization of the two levels of dialog,
mixing retrospective and present, adds to the confessional tone of the situation. The revelation of the

situation. The revelation of the identity of Jaguar in this manner, in the new role he has assumed, is consistent with the suspenseful, and mysterious aspect of the novel's structure.[5] An air of mystery surrounds the portrayal of Tere's childhood companion, who, ironically, is the same fierce Jaguar during adolescence. That the confessed murderer adjusts more readily to society than any of the other cadets is also ironic.

Another aspect of the suspensefulness of La ciudad y los perros is the fact that there is some doubt left in the reader's mind as to what actually happened to Arana. His death is one of the principal occurrences of the novel. Although Jaguar confesses to killing him, officially it is listed as an accident and the reader does not witness the shooting. This event, presented in an ambiguous manner, provides an opportunity to see how individuals and institutions react to complex situations. Thus irony as related to narrative technique plays an important part in the structure of La ciudad y los perros.

Alberto is involved to some extent in the author's ironic presentation of characters, as he prepares to inform Gamboa of the cadet's clandestine activities. The setting and situation are presented in an ironic manner as Alberto makes his phone call from a bar:

> "¿Teniente Gamboa?", pregunta Alberto.
> "Pisco de Montesierpe, afirma la sombra,
> mal pisco. Pisco Motocachi, buen pisco."
> "Yo soy. ¿Quién habla?" "Un cadete,"
> responde Alberto. "Un cadete de quinto
> año." Viva mi chola y vivan mis amigos.
> "¿Qué quiere?" "El mejor pisco del
> mundo, a mi entender, asegura la sombra.
> Pero rectifica. O uno de los mejores
> señor. Pisco Motocachi." "Su nombre",
> dice Gamboa. "Tendré diez hijos. Todos
> hombres. Para ponerles el nombre de
> cada uno de mis amigos, muchachos. El
> mío a ninguno, sólo los nombres de
> ustedes." "A Arana lo mataron dice
> Alberto. Yo sé quién fue. ¿Puede ir
> a su casa?" "Su nombre", dice Gamboa.
> "¿Quiere usted matar a una ballena?
> Déle pisco Motocachi, señor." (p. 239)

Interspersed with Alberto's action and dialog are

remarks from the bar patrons. Alberto's questions are associated with answers belonging to another conversation. In this instance the setting serves to trivialize Alberto's heroic act.

The irony of this situation involves an amount of humor, based on the bar talk, which is contrasted with the seriousness of Alberto's mission. This incongruous presentation of circumstances is indicative of the author's ironic technique. The juxtaposition of the different levels of speech, serious/comic, provides an implicit ironic comment.

Vargas Llosa's depiction of the military involves such elements of irony as humor, parody, ridicule, and sarcasm. At all levels of the chain of command, characters are presented with their shortcomings. Luis Díez makes the point that:

> . . . humor is greatly dependent on an ironic, disrespectful approach to themes and ideas of military life. The idea of the sanctity of duty in military life has always had a hollow sound to the layman. There is a thread of this anti-military irony running throughout the book.[6]

In La ciudad y los perros, ironic sequences of events and human actions are usually narrated from the point of view of the cadets. The fact that most of them do not want to be a part of the military system accounts, in part, for this attitude. The cadets are presented as being more apt than the system which is training them.

Aside from overt mockery of his military characters, Vargas Llosa's ironic technique involves a subtle type of foreshadowing which is also essential. For example, as Gamboa, for purposes of evidence, prepares to reenact the maneuvers in which Arana was killed the following scene is set. Mode of presentation is important in the depiction of the circumstances:

> La mañana seguía muy clara y había poca humedad. La brisa agitaba apenas la hierba del descampado; la vicuña ejecutaba veloces carreras en círculo. Pronto llegaría el verano; el colegio

> quedaría desierto, la vida se volvería
> muelle y agobiante; los servicios serían
> más cortos, menos rígidos, podría ir a la
> playa tres veces por semana. Su mujer ya
> estaría bien; llevarían al niño de paseo
> en un coche. Además, dispondría de tiempo
> para estudiar. Ocho meses, no era un plazo
> muy grande para preparar el examen. Decían
> que sólo habría veinte plazas para capitán.
> Y eran doscientos postulantes. (p. 261)

Gamboa, along with the narrator, dares to look into
the future. He is totally unaware of impending doom as
he feels at peace with nature in an almost pastoral
setting. Discord is evident, however, in the presence
of the displaced vicuña. On the edge of the storm
which he is about to create, Gamboa can think only of
peace, happiness and promotions. Choice of tense is
important here, as the author does not use future;
rather he employs the conditional, which suggests a
certain hesitancy. Ironically, this serenity never
arrives for Gamboa because of the manner in which he
handles the Arana affair. Tone is therefore also
important in the author's ironic portrayal of Gamboa.

The Colonel is usually presented in ironic terms
in both his speech and actions. But his serious
nature is shown at the end of his lecture to Alberto
who has accused Jaguar of murder:

> La próxima vez, antes de jugar al
> detective, piense que está en el Ejér-
> cito, una institución donde los super-
> iores vigilan para que todo sea debida-
> mente investigado y sancionado. Puede
> irse. (p. 287)

The fact that this speech is being made to Alberto,
who by exposing the amount of illegal goods in the
barracks, has just shown how incompetently the officers
"vigilan" the cadets, is ironic. The same method of
accountability has been employed in the coverup of
the Arana incident and forms a part of the built-in
military inefficiency.

In La ciudad y los perros irony is present from
the depiction of daily routine to the very structure
and function of the military. This is achieved through
characterization, mode of presentation, situational
development, and technique being employed as vehicles

35

of irony. The contradictions, incongruities, and incompatibilities which form the basis of verbal and dramatic irony form an integral part of the internal structure of La ciudad y los perros. However, in this novel the author's manipulation of irony has not achieved the depth prevalent in his later works.

LA CASA VERDE

It is perhaps in La casa verde where we best observe the "irony of events," a variation of dramatic irony, at work on the outcome of individual destinies. The trajectories of Lituma, Nieves, Fushía, and Padre García exemplify the tendency toward unpredictable encounters, which are so important in the structure of Vargas Llosa's novels. The author's narrative presentation involves an intertwining of destinies which accentuates the similarities of individual struggles. His literary protagonists appear to be floundering in a series of ironic occurrences which dramatize aspects of the human condition.

The same inconsistency of character observed in Jaguar is present also in Lituma, who is shown in La casa verde to embody various contradictions as an individual. Lituma, or "el Sargento," is one of the characters who shares in both the jungle and urban experiences. Critics who find it difficult to reconcile the two images of Lituma which are presented in La casa verde exaggerate, I think, when they blame the author's technique of withholding information. As in the case of the adolescents in La ciudad y los perros, Lituma, too, reaches a type of self realization as the reader discovers who Lituma really is. The author combines technique and theme to render an ironic presentation of the process of self definition. There are sufficient clues presented throughout to convincingly link the two sides of Lituma. The contradictions in his character are based on the difference between the role Lituma is forced to play when surrounded by the mangaches and his true nature which is revealed when he is alone.

For example, when we first come into contact with Lituma in Santa María on an individual level he seems to be plagued with doubts. This is made explicit as he keeps reassuring himself upon approaching Nieves' house in search of Bonifacia. He asks himself, "¿era o no era un mangache?, ¿dónde se la había ido la braveza?"[7] The old spirit is still there but not

36

in the belligerent manner which is characteristic of
the inconquistables. Lituma is different from his
immediate friends in that he does have gainful employ-
ment and self respect. There are several sides to
Lituma who represents the macho type, a concept which
embodies an air of dignity. He shows this dimension
of his character in the early relationship with
Bonifacia, whom he really loves.

On the other hand, Lituma is forced to act
because of pride when Seminario, in Piura, incessantly
challenges his manhood. Lituma suggests a game of
Russian roulette in which Seminario is killed. Out
of self respect Lituma is forced to act, defend his
hombría, or manhood. But the fact that Seminario is
one of the leading citizens forces Lituma to go to
jail where he loses a lifetime which cannot be regained.
As he leaves for prison in Lima, Josefino, one of the
mangaches, is already making plans for Bonifacia's
future. One irrational act on the part of Lituma in
defense of his hombría ironically causes him to
lose it.

After his spell in jail Lituma returns to find
Bonifacia working with la Chunga, which is a terrible
blow to his ego. He seeks revenge by beating up
Josefino and Bonifacia, who had urged Lituma to get
revenge on the former:

> Pero en vez de hacerle caso, Lituma
> se volvió contra ella, la tumbó en
> la arena de un empujón y la estuvo
> pateando, puta, arrastrada, siete leches,
> insultándola hasta que perdió la
> voz y las fuerzas. Entonces se dejó
> caer en la arena y empezó a sollozar
> como un churre. (p. 190)

This is indeed a strange reaction for an
inconquistable such as Lituma. Until his discovery
of Bonifacia's new position he had managed to maintain,
even through jail, the pride and dignity which is
characteristic of machismo. Now, however, there is
very little which separates him from the other
inconquistables. Upon their return to the brothel,
Bonifacia tries to free herself from a demanding
customer but Lituma consents to the fact that Bonifacia
is indeed a prostitute and he cannot change it.
Recently out of jail, he has nothing to offer, thus

accepting in body and spirit what the inconquistables really pretend to be. The fact that they came to Piura with high aspirations is now of no importance. Lituma has encountered the destiny which he attempted to avoid. The goals for which he aspired and his achievements are very much incompatible.

The case of Adrián Nieves will serve as another example to show how striking the irony of interpersonal relationships is in Vargas Llosa's novels. These ironic coincidences, which the reader encounters so often, are related to his technique of relating lives and experiences in almost unbelievable ways. Thus the author emphasizes the role of chance and accident in shaping the course of individual histories.

Initially forced to flee the civil guard, where he serves as guide, to avoid being killed by Indians, Nieves is rescued by Fushía whom he betrays by escaping with Lalita. Over the years Nieves manages to raise a family and forget about his past activities. However, when Pantacha, the only survivor of Fushía's band, is discovered on the island he incriminates Nieves. The person who is in charge of making the arrest is none other than the sergeant who was first introduced to Bonifacia by Nieves. As he contemplates whether or not to flee Nieves surmises:

> --Me tendrán adentro unos meses pero
> después ya viviré tranquilo y podré
> volver aquí--dijo Adrián Nieves--.
> Si me meto al monte no veré nunca más
> a mi mujer ni a mis hijos, y no
> quiero vivir como un animal hasta que
> me muera. Yo no maté a nadie, eso
> le consta al Pantacha, a los paganos.
> Aquí me he portado como un buen
> cristiano. (p. 336)

This is the last knowledge we acquire concerning Nieves from his point of view. He is content to spend a short time in prison because in reality he has not done anything wrong. But somebody has to pay for the atrocities which Fushía has committed and Nieves happens to be most accessible. The law, in this case, is indiscriminate--innocence is secondary.

In the epilog we learn that Lalita has maintained her curiosity about the whereabouts of Nieves. Although

she is now married to Pesado, she inquires through her
son Aquilino who now lives in Iquitos. His reply is:

> --Se habrá ido al Brasil --dice Aqui-
> lino--. Los que salen de la cárcel se
> van a Manaos. Aquí no les dan trabajo.
> El habrá conseguido allá, si es que era
> tan buen práctico como cuentan. Sólo
> que tanto tiempo lejos del río, a lo
> mejor se le olvidó el oficio. (pp. 403-4)

The "irony of events" whereby Nieves encounters the
destiny which he set out to avoid is driven home by
Aquilino. Nieves is now in exile, without family or
friends, completely destroyed by the sequence of occur-
ences. What he anticipated to be a short-term prison
sentence resulted in his losing everthing, including
his talent as guide. Given a set of alternatives,
Nieves makes the wrong decision, as do most of Vargas
Llosa's characters. For him, going to jail brings the
same result as if he had taken refuge in the jungle.
Nieves unknowingly takes precisely the steps that
lead him away from his goal.

The fact that Vargas Llosa's characters find
themselves in impossible situations is no mere artistic coincidence. Rather it is the author's way of
presenting the difficulties of their fight for survival. We, as readers, are able to perceive much more
than the characters themselves, which results in
their predicament being more pronounced. We see individuals entrapped by their circumstances without
means of salvation.

Fushía is an example of this inability to overcome
circumstances as early in the novel he flees from
Reátegui with Lalita but to Reátegui's stronghold
in Uchamala. He spends the rest of his life as a
fugitive. Just before the final powerful scene of his
disintegration, Fushía and Aquilino end their conversation on a comment oriented, ironically, towards the
future. In his plight it is not probable that Fushía
will endure another year. Aquilino's final words are
intended to be optimistic:

> --No te pongas triste Fushía --mur-
> mura--. Vendré el otro año, aunque esté
> muy cansado, mi palabra. Te traeré
> cosas blanditas. ¿Te enojaste por lo
> de Lalita? ¿Te acordaste de otros
> tiempos? Así es la vida, hombre, al

menos te fue mejor que a otros, fíjate
Nieves. (p. 390)

Fushía is in the worst imaginable shape, even if it is
the lesser of two evils, as evidenced by the comparison with Nieves. Even he is aware of the fact that
Aquilino does not mean what he is saying, and that
his aim is to pacify. But Fushía clings to the future
which, in reality, does not exist for him. Fushía
is left helpless in a hostile, indifferent natural world
which has no concern for his plight.

The moral battle between Padre García and Anselmo,
which lasted several decades also ends with an ironic
twist. Padre García, who is known in the Mangachería
as "quemador", or burner, of the Green House and who
has for years been ostracized by the residents, returns
to officiate the last rites of Anselmo. He feels
that the other priest is not qualified. Thus the long
rivalry between Anselmo and García ends on a positive
note. Although the priest has not basically changed
his opinion concerning Anselmo and things in general,
García shows a certain amount of respect for his moral
obligation to the community. This supersedes his
tough attitude towards the mangaches, which is dealt
with in a humorous way in Vargas Llosa's characterization of him. The incongruities presented are indicative of the complex nature of this individual.

La casa verde, which is structured around numerous
voyages and chance occurrences, is thematically concerned with the nature and importance of human choices.
The decisions made by the characters such as Lituma,
Nieves, and Fushía, seem to them, to be based on
sound logic at the moment when they make them, but
they result, ironically, in adversity or a clash with
ideals.

CONVERSACION EN LA CATEDRAL

In its historical dimension Conversación en La
Catedral examines the Odría era in Peru. Narrated
from the points of view of a dissident and an outcast,
the novel presents a critical view of the period. A
look at how one of these characters, Ambrosio, reacts
to his situation and the ironic manner in which he is
at times presented will reveal much about critical
authorial attitudes concerning the human condition in
Peru. Both dramatic and cosmic irony are factors in
Ambrosio's characterization as revealed in his

40

relationship with Trifulcio, Queta and himself.

The episode of Trifulcio's death in this novel and Ambrosio's reaction to his personal plight, is probably the best example of the fusion of these two types of irony in Vargas Llosa's works. Trifulcio, Ambrosio's father, is freed from prison in order to serve in the senatorial campaign of Arévalo. Trifulcio's brief furlough to his home in Chincha results in rejection by Tomasa, his wife. Trifulcio follows the campaign trail, as body guard and counter demonstrator, to a tragic end in Arequipa during a demonstration which leads to a major shakeup in the Odría regime.

This incident is recalled by Ambrosio as it was related to him by Ludovico Pantoja, Trifulcio's partner, who was wounded when they tried to break up the demonstration:

> --Nos dividieron en grupos de a dos--
> dijo Ludovico--. A Hipólito y a mí
> nos separaron.
> --Ludovico Pantoja con el negro--dijo
> Molina--. ¿Trifulcio, no?
> --Me dieron de yunta al que andaba hecho
> polvo por el soroche--dijo Ludovico--.
> Uno de los que mataron en el teatro.
> Fíjate si no me pasó cerca, Ambrosio.
> --Son veintidós, once parejitas--dijo
> Molina--. Reconózcanse bien, no se
> vayan a confundir.
> --Nos mataron tres y a catorce nos
> mandaron al hospital--dijo Ludovico--.
> Y el cobarde de Hipólito ileso, dime
> si es justo.
> --Quiero ver si han entendido--dijo
> Molina--. A ver, tú, repíteme lo que
> vas a hacer.
> El que iba a ser su pareja le pasó
> la botella y Trifulcio tomó un trago:
> gusanitos que corrían por su cuerpo y
> calor. Trifulcio le estiró la mano:
> tanto gusto, ¿a él siendo de Lima la
> altura no le había hecho nada? Nada,
> dijo Ludovico, y se sonrieron.[8]

Ambrosio innocently accepts the set of circumstances without having the slightest notion of their implication. Deception is essential in the technique employed

to recount this episode. The author has arranged the
narrative so that Ambrosio exposes himself in his
ironic predicament to the reader. The incongruity of
this situation lies in the contrast between the meaning
intended by Ludovico and the added significance of the
manner of presentation of Molina and Trifulcio as
seen by the reader. This underscores Ambrosio's
ignorance.

In this retrospective presentation of the
disastrous Arequipa episode Ambrosio is portrayed as
the victim of an unjust set of ironic circumstances.
He has no way of knowing that his own father was
killed in the episode. This ironic detachment on the
author's part is maintained by the interspersing of
parallel dialogs separated in time and space. On one
level Ludovico is talking with Ambrosio; on another
Molina is planning battle strategy; and on still
another plane there is the exchange between Trifulcio
and Ludovico as they prepare to do battle. Remote
past, past, and Ambrosio's recollection in the present
combine to structure the irony of the situation.

During this particular episode, Trifulcio, who
throughout the novel is characterized as being just
one step above the non-human level, is shown to be
concerned also about his position in the universe. On
several occasions, he thinks of home and he does not
appear to still have the old killer instinct. Trifulcio is suffering from soroche, altitude sickness, and
aware of his aging.[9] But for him there is no escape
because everybody shows complete indifference toward
his plight. While the savage battle rages inside the
theater, Trifulcio reaches a point where all he wants
is "aire" but his feverish efforts to get it are
thwarted as he is beaten and suffocates like an animal.
From the moment Trifulcio first appears in the novel
until his death he appears terribly alone in his plight,
an instrument to be used and abused by others.

The fact that Trifulcio was aware of greater
human problems besides sex, eating, sleeping, and
drinking is dramatized in subtle ways by Vargas Llosa.
Outer appearance and inner reality are shown to be
two contradictory aspects of his being. The deeper
interpretation of both Trifulcio's and Ambrosio's
plight is made by the latter upon his return to Chincha
from Lima. Alone, without friends or roots, and
lacking even the knowledge of where his family is
buried Ambrosio reflects:

> Se había acordado de algo que le
> dijo Trifulcio esa noche, la víspera
> de su partida a Lima, cuando caminaban
> a oscuras: estoy en Chincha y siento
> que no estoy, reconozco todo y no
> reconozco nada. Ahora entendía lo
> que había querido decirle. (II, p. 307)

Completely alienated, Ambrosio now feels that he
understands better the purposelessness of his life.
But just as with Trifulcio before him, nobody has
attempted to understand his situation. Ambrosio's
trajectory, too, has been a complete cycle which led
to nothing. Rootless, he has roamed the earth without
leaving any recognizable impression.

This realization represents the height of
metaphysical irony which according to Glicksberg
"becomes tragic when it seeks to give imaginative
expression to the discovery that the universe has
no concern at all for the fate of man."[10] Both men
have been aware of the social and ethnic realities
of their problem but to feel that the cosmos, too, is
totally indifferent is a tragic blow. The author's
negative ironic presentation of these two characters
helps to accentuate great problems inherent in their
situations as black Peruvians.

One of the implicit ironies in the Trifulcio-
Ludovico-Ambrosio relationship is that during the
Arequipa confrontation in which Trifulcio is killed,
Ludovico, his partner, is identified with the wrong
forces, which eventually leads to his becoming a part
of the system of corruption and rewards.

Symbolically Trifulcio is sacrificed for this
purpose. Yet after the murder of Hortensia, Ambrosio
has to bribe Ludovico in order to escape to Pucallpa.
Ludovico arranges his exile knowing that Ambrosio is
no match for don Hilario, Ludovico's cousin, who
succeeds in relieving Ambrosio of his money. In
Conversación en La Catedral the novel is structured
to show characters caught in many different ironic
situations as the complexities of human interactions
are explored, often with tragic endings.

Queta, the prostitute-lesbian in the novel offers
in an ironic way views which are symptomatic of the
class structure and social attitudes in general. Though

43

a mere prostitute by profession because she is mulata, she considers herself superior to Ambrosio because of his blackness. Typically, she denies this but still charges him ridiculous prices for her favors. A part of their meetings over two years is devoted to mental torture as exemplified in the following conversation in which they discuss the Fermín-Ambrosio homosexual relationship:

> --Me gusta ser su chofer--dijo Ambrosio--.
> Tengo mi cuarto, gano más que antes, y
> todos me tratan con consideración.
> --¿Y cuando se baja los pantalones y te
> dice cumple tus obligaciones?--se
> rió Queta--. ¿Te gusta también?
> --No es lo que usted cree--repitió
> Ambrosio, despacio--. Yo sé que
> usted se imagina. Falso, no es así.
> --¿Y cuando te da asco?--dijo Queta--.
> A veces a mí me da, pero qué importa,
> abro las piernas y es igual. ¿Pero
> tú? (II, p. 226)

Queta continues to drive home her point by repeating "sólo abro las piernas" and "¿Pero tú?". It seems strange that a person who has run the gamut of sexual relations as she has done would assume such a pious attitude.

Generally speaking, homosexuality between women is no different than homosexuality between men. In this case Queta's attitude is based completely on Ambrosio's ethnic background when, ironically, they are both in the same plight. Although she tries to build up the Fermín-Ambrosio affair as a master-slave relationship, her homosexual episodes with Hortensia for the voyeuristic purposes of Cayo Bermúdez are based on the same principle. Given a particular set of social attitudes, they are shown to be at work in the most unexpected quarters. At any rate, their final destinies are similar as Queta returns to the whorehouse and ambrosio to the dog pound.

After their four-hour conversation Santiago is concerned about what Ambrosio will do when his stint in the dog pound has ended. The pessimistic reply is:

> Trabajaría aquí, allá, a lo mejor
> dentro de un tiempo habría otra epidemia
> de rabia y lo llamarían de nuevo, y después

aquí, allá, y después, bueno, después
ya se moriría ¿no, niño? (II, p. 309)

Choice of tense and language is important here as it
serves to underscore Ambrosio's plight. The language
game he plays in answering Santiago's question is only
a small part of the larger game his life's plan has
been. The use of conditional once again points out
the hesitancy about the future. Throughout Conversación en La Catedral the feeling pervades that Ambrosio
is a victim of circumstances. It will always be
the Ambrosios and Trifulcios who are called upon to
be exploited in times of rabia, be it animal (rabies)
or human (rage).

Part of the incongruity of Ambrosio's existence
stems from the fact that he is presented as a type of
scapegoat in Conversación en La Catedral. As Northrop
Frye points out in his assessment of the ironic
predicament of the scapegoat,

> The pharmakos is neither innocent
> nor guilty. He is innocent in the
> sense that what happens to him is
> far greater than anything that he
> has done provokes. . . . He is
> guilty in the sense that he is a
> member of a guilty society or living
> in a world where such injustices are
> an inescapable part of existence.[11]

Ambrosio is a victim, innocent/guilty, precisely
because he is a black Peruvian who must suffer the
consequences of discrimination and oppression within
a society which places more value on skin color than
on true worth. The duality of his character is evident
on both a social and on an existential level. As
presented in this novel, Ambrosio is overwhelmed by
the multiple aspects of reality which confront him.

PANTALEON Y LAS VISITADORAS

Dramatic and verbal irony form the structural
basis of Pantaleón y las visitadoras. These devices
are evident in the presentation of Pocha, Pantaleón
and brother Francisco. Thematically, however, serious
questions are raised concerning blind devotion to
a cause.

45

In Pantaleón y las visitadoras a basically comic
novel, most of the characters find themselves at one
time or another caught in some dramatically ironic
situation. An example of this is the incident where
Pochita is leaving Pantaleón because of his activities
with prostitutes. As she arrives at the airport with
her friend, Alicia, Sinchi requests an interview.
Although Pochita refuses, in the process she says all
that is necessary without realizing that she is
being recorded:

> --Pero qué quiere usted aquí todavía,
> oye Alicia, qué tipo tan cargoso.
> ¿No le he dicho que no le voy a dar
> ningún reportaje sobre mi marido?
> Que no lo será por mucho tiempo,
> además, porque te juro Alicia, llegando
> a Lima voy donde el abogado y le
> planteo el divorcio. A ver si no me
> dan la custodia de Gladycita con las
> porquerías que está haciendo aquí
> ese desgraciado.12

Her seemingly innocent conversation provides el
Sinchi with plenty of damaging evidence against
Pantaleón. Most of the characters in the novel are
naively destructive, either to themselves or to others.
Pantaleón himself is the prime example of this tendency.
Pocha, however, allows for more comic ironic situations.

One of the truly outstanding comic moments of the
novel comes when Pochita writes her sister a letter
about a certain incident which she experienced with
lavanderas (prostitutes who pose as washerwomen). In
need of a maid, Pocha is constantly harassed by women
offering to do laundry and she finally approaches one:

> Le grité espérese un ratito, me
> levanté en camisón y salí a abrirle
> la puerta. Ahí mismo debí sospechar
> que pasaba algo raro porque la niña
> tenía pinta de todo menos lavandera,
> pero yo, una boba, en la luna. Una
> huachafita de lo más presentable,
> cinchada para resaltar las curvas por
> supuesto, con las uñas pintadas y muy
> arregladita. Me miró de arriba abajo,
> de lo más asombrada y yo pensé que le
> pasa a ésta, que tengo para que me
> miré así. Le dije entre, ella se metió

> a la casa y antes de que le dijese nada
> vio la puerta del dormitorio y a Panta
> en la cama y pum se lanzó derechita, y,
> sin más ni más, se planteó frente a tu
> cuñado en una pose que me dejó bizca,
> la mano en la cadera y las piernas
> abiertas como gallito que va a atacar.
> Panta se sentó en la cama de un salto,
> se le salían los ojos de asombro por
> la aparición de la mujer. ¿Y que te
> crees que hizo la tipa antes de que
> yo o Panta atináramos a decirle espere
> afuera, qué hace aquí en el dormitorio?
> Empezó a hablar de la tarifa, me tienen
> que pagar el doble, que ella no
> acostumbra ocuparse con mujeres, seña-
> lándome a mí, flaca, cáete muerta,
> para darse estos gustos hay que chancar
> y no sé que vulgaridades y de repente
> me di cuenta del enredo y me empezaron
> a temblar las piernas. (p. 78)

This lengthy quote preserves the true sense of the situation in which Pocha found herself. The incongrui-ty is revealed in an initial miscommunication between the two women. This is compounded by the horrified reaction of Pocha to the idea of sexual relations between two women, an attitude incompatible with her conception of sex and the family.

Vargas Llosa captures artistically Pocha's recreation of the incident with all its humorous implications. Use of the letter form to show Pocha's obvious innocence enhances her confessional air as she, this time, is victim of a comic/ironic situation. Thus in Pocha's case we are shown both tragic and comic manifestations of the incongruities of her existence in the divorce incident with Sinchi and with the lavandera.

Comic elements are counterbalanced by the serious implications of situations presented in the novel. This is especially evident in the exchange between Pantaleón and his mother concerning the gravity of the situation which has developed after Pantaleón publicly eulogizes la Brasileña:

> --No lamento nada de lo que he
> hecho . . . He actuado según mi
> conciencia y ese también es el deber

47

de un soldado. Haré frente a lo
que venga. Ten confianza en mí,
mamá.
--Siempre la he tenido, hijito--lo
escobilla, lo lustra, lo arregla,
abre los brazos, lo besa, lo aprieta,
mira a los bigotudos del viejo retrato
la señora Leonor--. Una fe ciega
en ti. Pero con este asunto ya no
sé que pensar. Te volviste loco,
Panta. ¡Vestirse de militar para
pronunciar un discurso en el entie-
rro de una pe! ¿Tu padre, tu abuelo
hubieran hecho una cosa así? (p. 278)

Pantaleón obviously does not take into account
right and wrong when he follows his conscience which
places in jeopardy a family tradition in the military.
Señora Leonor makes this point in her manipulation of
the picture, presumably of his father. Pantaleón
elevates la Brasileña to the same stature of the
military personnel in his family by his eulogy which
goes against all logic. The fact that he is following
his beliefs does not necessarily change the difficult
situation which he has created for himself by a series
of irrational acts. Ironically, he is not able to
deviate from his chosen path. Thus the military
mentality of Pantaleón and the "religion" of el
Hermano, in the quest for converts to his cult, are
presented by the author as being different variations
of fanaticism.

The tragic ending of Hermano Francisco exemplifies
one of the most shocking ironies of Pantaleón y las
visitadoras. An advocate of sacrificing various types
of animals on the cross, Francisco himself is forever
on the run and finally captured by the army, kidnapped
by followers, and crucified. Francisco's fate is
recounted from several points of view, with most of
his final actions as told by his followers being pure
fantasy. However, both his constituents and the
military do agree that he ended in the river.

Much of the second-hand information is being
relayed by prostitutes and by Milcaras, who has a tendency to exaggerate, as the name, Thousand Faces, suggests. Francisco, who undoubtedly looked forward to
being the martyr of a great movement, ends as a putrid
mass of flesh in the river. His juxtapositioning with
Pantaleón highlights the similarities between the

48

"Mission" of the two and their willingness to adhere to their beliefs at all costs. As Gustavo Alvarez points out"

> La hábil manera de contraponer al capitán de intendencia Pantaleón Pantoja y al hermano Fracisco, el hermano del Arca, que consigue adeptos para su religión con la misma facilidad con que los consigue Pantoja con sus visitadoras, establece una similitud irónica entre la religión y la vida militar.[13]

The army, mindful of the explosiveness of the Francisco situation, handled it in an expedient manner by simply eliminating a potential symbol of fanaticism. Both Francisco and Pantaleón, who strove for greatness, end in defeat.

The ironic structure of Vargas Llosa's novels encompasses three basic contradictions. First of all, the experiences examined reveal a conflict between what is expected and what, in effect, is achieved. Secondly, there is a contradiction between values and aspirations and what characters ultimately accomplish. In addition, the discrepancy between what is evident on the surface and the implications of a given situation is paramount to our understanding of the narrative.

Vargas Llosa, as novelist, creates ambiguous situations which are in turn given various interpretations by different mentalities as they seek to make their existence meaningful. In this respect, D. C. Muecke writes:

> (Irony is) a view of life which recognizes that experience is open to multiple interpretations, of which no one is simply right, and that the co-existence of incongruities is a part of the structure of existence.[14]

In Vargas llosa's fictional world reality is shown to be complex and subjected to different character interpretations whereby the important thing is to make life meaningful. In this sense Vargas Llosa sees Peruvian man as victim of an irony inherent in the human condition. The total experience in Peru is one in which appearance is very much out of proportion with reality.

There is a constant contrast between the individual's conscious aspirations and what society eventually makes of him. This is evident in terms of the education of the boys in La ciudad y los perros, the attempt to achieve social acceptability in Conversación en La Catedral, the effort to redefine military efficiency in Pantaleón y las visitadoras, and in the attempt to make the correct choices in La casa verde.

The inconsistencies and incongruities in modes of characterization and presentation are compatible with Vargas Llosa's ironic view that the world in its essence is paradoxical and that an ambivalent presentation alone can grasp its contradictions. In order to perceive the totality of a situation or an experience, different points of view and interpretations are necessary; thus the shifting points of view and interiorization in the novels, which reinforce the ironic presentation of characters.

In La ciudad y los perros, La casa verde, Conversación en La Catedral, and Pantaleón y las visitadoras irony is one of the basic ingredients in our perception of theme, structure, characterization, style, and world view. Manifestations of this concept occur verbally, dramatically, and metaphysically. In Vargas Llosa's interpretation of Peruvians and their institutions a many sided focus is employed which allows him to present situations which, instead of being over-simplified, are compatible with the built-in contradictions found in human experience.

NOTES

[1]Alex Preminger, ed., Encyclopedia of Poetry and Poetics (Princeton: Princeton University Press, 1965), p. 407. This corresponds to interpretations of irony set forth by Wellek in Chapter 1 of his History of Modern Criticism: 1750-1950 (New Haven: Yale University Press, 1955) and Northrop Frye, Anatomy of Criticism (Princeton: Princeton University Press, 1957), various sections are devoted to irony.

[2]Charles Glicksberg, The Ironic Vision in Modern Literature (The Hague: Martinus Nijhoff, 1969), p. II.

[3]"There is only one minor criticism one would make, and that is a gross coincidence in the plot, over-weighted by dramatic irony, whereby the slave and his chief tormentor both love the same girl, unbeknown to the other."
"No Formentor," rev. of La ciudad y los perros, Times Literary Supplement, January 9, 1974, p. 21.

[4]Mario Vargas Llosa, La ciudad y los perros (7th ed.; Barcelona: Seix Barral, 1971), p. 89. Cited hereafter in text.

[5]Point discussed by several critics, "Sobre La ciudad y los perros," Casa de las Américas (La Habana, Cuba), Año 5, No. 30 (mayo-junio 1965), 63-80.

[6]Luis Díez, Mario Vargas Llosa's Pursuit of the Total Novel (Cuernavaca, Mexico: CIDOC, 1970), p. I-105.

[7]Mario Vargas Llosa, La casa verde (11th ed.; Barcelona: Seix Barral, 1971), p. 174. Cited hereafter in text.

[8]Mario Vargas Llosa, Conversación en La Catedral, 2 vols. (5th ed.; Barcelona: Seix Barral, 1971), II, 137-8. Cited hereafter in text.

[9]Although soroche is recognized as a common illness associated with altitude, here it is related to Trifulcio's ethnic background and a Peruvian stereotype. "'Gallinazo no canta en puna' dice el refrán limeño y es efectivo que el negro no ha logrado instalarse en las serranías." Anibal Ismodes Cairo, Sociología del Perú (2nd ed.; Lima: Rocarme, 1969), p. 52.

[10]Glicksberg, p. 12

[11]Frye, p. 41.

[12]Mario Vargas Llosa, Pantaleón y las visitadoras (Barcelona: Seix Barral, 1973), p. 203. Cited hereafter in text.

[13]Gustavo Alvarez Gardeazabal, "La novela hispano-americana: García Márquez y Vargas Llosa," Indice, Año 5, No. 30 (1 noviembre 1973), 51.

[14]D. C. Muecke, Irony (London: Methuen, 1970), p. 22.

CHAPTER 3

DETERMINISM AND EXISTENTIALISM: A DIFFICULT AMALGAM

Determinism

Critics have been unable to come to an agreement about whether a determinist view of the human condition underlies the major novels of Mario Vargas Llosa.   In this analysis of the problem, the focus will be the manner in which psychological, sociological, environmental, historical and political forces are presented in these novels and the significance they acquire in the destinies of the major characters.   The apparent contradiction between determinism and existentialism, another doctrine influential in Vargas Llosa's works, will also be treated.   The objective here is to show how the two contradictory doctrines combine in the author's works to express a coherent view of the human condition.

In his study, <u>Mario Vargas Llosa: la invención de una realidad</u>, José Miguel Oviedo summarizes arguments advanced by Boldori, McMurray, Harss, Pacheco, Edwards and Vargas Llosa himself concerning the alleged <u>determinismo</u> of the latter.   However, Oviedo does not reach a conclusion about this matter: rather he takes a neutral approach by stating:

> Aclaremos que no estamos negando de plano que el aspecto determinista realmente exista; lo que queremos señalar es que, justamente, gracias a esa visión que preferimos llamar <u>fatalista</u> (el determinismo sugiere una simplificación causal; el fatalismo, la oscura ramificación de los móviles humanos) sus novelas extraen su potencia y su valor trascendente, su pasión y su belleza. Vargas Llosa no les niega a sus personajes la libertad; si en sus narraciones aparecen como arrastrados por fuerzas superiores a ellos, es porque han <u>elegido</u> ya muchas veces su propio destino, lo han aceptado como un reto: no es la falta de opciones sino el furioso agotamiento de ellas lo que distingue sus vidas y las sella.[1]

53

Ironically, this argument, despite Oviedo's intent, is more in favor of determinism than fatalism. Oviedo's discussion continues along these lines, linking Vargas Llosa with other authors and finally to Jean-Paul Sartre. However, in attempting to minimize the theory of determinism Oviedo has chosen the alternate doctrine of fatalism. Perhaps a definition of the two terms would help to clarify the matter.

In the introduction to his book, <u>Determinism, Freewill and Moral Responsibility</u>, Gerald Dworkin remarks that there are:

> . . . two fundamental ingredients of any determinism: a belief in universal causal laws and a notion of predictability. . . . Determinism should not be confused with what might be called predeterminism, or fatalism. Fatalism states that our output is not affected by any efforts or decisions that we make. This is a stronger claim than determinism, in effect not only claiming that our outputs are caused, but also specifying certain factors as being causally irrelevant to the outcome.[2]

Dowrkin's definition and distinction between the two concepts are compatible with those advanced by most scholars who have treated the subject. According to the doctrine of fatalism, future events will occur regardless of the prevailing causal conditions at that time. There appears to be a confusion of terms by Oviedo which does not help to alleviate the built-in contradictions which we find in the works of Mario Vargas Llosa.

Determinism, with emphasis on causality and predictability, is distinguishable from fatalism by the mere fact that being caused is not the same as being compelled. Causality deals with events outside the sphere of the individual control, while predictability works on the assumption that given a set of options man will make a particular choice. This is not the same as stating that events will occur regardless of what one does.

Determinism, then, is the theory that there are forces which govern human actions. However, determinism allows room for human efforts and decisions and takes into account their relevance to the ultimate outcome of the events. Since the novelist is not directly concerned with abstract philosophy (although it may be observed in his world view), the doctrine will be manifested in his work in theme and character presentation.

A summary of the basic philosophical questions surrounding the free will/determinism controversy will show that the problem is far from being resolved. According to Edward D'Angelo, whose definitions of determinism and fatalism are compatible with Dworkin's but who extends his distinctions even further by defining certain categories:

> There are four possible positions that can be taken in the free will controversy. First, the belief that determinism is false and freedom is true. This position is known as libertarianism. Second, the belief that both determinism and freedom are true; determinism is compatible with the notion of freedom. This position is known as soft determinism. Third, the belief that determinism is true and freedom is false. This is the position of the hard determinist. Fourth, the belief that both determinism and freedom are false.[3]

D'Angelo's assessment of the four possible positions which can be taken in the free will controversy will be useful for the purposes of the study.

Based on my reading and interpretation of the best of the critics, the concept of "soft determinism" will be used in this study as the working hypothesis for an understanding of how Vargas Llosa uses the deterministic world view. Seen in this light, his outlook on life may be considered pessimistic but certainly not fatalistic. The fatalist, who maintains that man's desires and choices are irrelevant and that all events, being beyond human control, will occur in a predetermined way which cannot be changed by man's will or choice, seems to reflect an attitude different from that taken by Vargas Llosa. With "soft determinism," causality and predictability are important factors in man's destiny; however, he is considered free to make his own choices and is not completely overwhelmed by outside forces. Also, "soft determinism" holds man morally responsible for his acts since he exercises his options in an uncompelled manner.

Now that the distinction between fatalism and determinism has, hopefully, been made clear, and working definitions of determinism and "soft determinism" have been established, we can arrive more easily at an understanding of Vargas Llosa's characters. It will also be possible to examine whether his determinism can be reconciled with the existential basis or interpretation of his world view which is expressed in some of his major novels. In this regard his affinity for Sartre, which has been pointed out by many critics, will be discussed.

In attempting to analyze the novels of Vargas Llosa from a determinist perspective, there are two possible literary manifestations of the concept of determinism which can be taken into account. They are:

> . . . (a) the belief that men's choices
> are largely caused by irrational feelings,
> instinctual drives, or the unconscious
> (Zola, Dreiser, Lawrence); and (b) the
> belief that men's choices play little
> or no part in determining what happens
> to them, since their decisions are over-
> whelmed by natural or social forces
> (Hardy).[4]

Both these patterns involve "a particular theory of what is involved in the causation, and the outcome, of heroic choices." This general assessment is related to the unheroic and the introspective tendencies of modern fiction, both prominent factors in Vargas Llosa's narrative. The unheroic is the discernable mode in the dominance of social forces over man, while the introspective narration highlights irrational thoughts, feelings, and instinctual drives.

LA CIUDAD Y LOS PERROS

The historical, political, social, psychological, and environmental factors which tend to influence the outcome of the life trajectories of Vargas Llosa's characters fluctuate from novel to novel, thus precluding a narrow simplification of his works. While different novels offer different and better examples of these factors, it is important to see how they work first of all in <u>La ciudad y los perros</u>. Rosa Boldori's contention is that:

> La postulación esencial de la novela, en el plano de su fundamentación ideo- lógica, consiste en la imposibilidad del hombre de superar los condiciona- mientos del medio social y geográfico, en su <u>determinismo ambiental</u>. Esta posición se apoya en un materialismo histórico basado en el reconocimiento de la existencia de una realidad ajena al hombre, que le impone sus propias pautas opuestas a los intereses, proyectos y fantasías individuales. Queda descartada la utopía del libre albedrío, la posición del héroe romántico, culminado por el contrario el anonadamiento de los personajes bajo una máquina social monstruosa, Kafkiana, cuyos fines se desconocen o, simplemente no existen. Esta circunstancia despoja a los protagonistas de todo rasgo heroico, los devuelve a su limitada condición de hombres humillados, condenados a vivir sin pensar, a hundirse en la costumbre.[5]

While some of what Boldori says concerning the social conditioning of man and the absence of romantic heroism appears to be true, her position regarding "la utopía del libre albedrío" and "una realidad ajena al hombre," is somewhat untenable. Vargas Llosa's characters do make their own choices even if they are limited, and their basic problem relates to a human reality. Given a number of choices, Vargas Llosa's man will invariably make the wrong one.

Regardless of whether one believes that man is manipulated by forces beyond his control, we must realize that in any society there are certain elemental roles which an individual will perform. These range from the basic necessities, through interpersonal relationships, to decisions about goals and purpose in life. Surely an individual will adapt to society if he wants to survive within it, be it on society's terms or on his own. In the novels of Mario Vargas

Llosa one can clearly see the forces which influence
the formulation and final destinies of his characters.
A careful analysis will reveal to a large extent
their motivations.

In La ciudad y los perros the boys are sent to
the Leoncio Prado so that they may become men and
be molded into good citizens. Throughout the entire
educational process, as the cadets pass through
adolescence, there are moments of rebellion against
the rules of society, but the end product is always
the same. The young men are schooled in society's
mores and readied to perpetuate the system.

Distinguishable among the cadets are Alberto,
Ricardo, and Jaguar, representing middle, lower middle,
and lower classes, respectively. Alberto and Ricardo
are identified early in the novel and can be observed
throughout, while Jaguar's identity is not revealed
until the latter part. They all have common ground
in the form of relations with Teresa, with whom each
one is in love during his career. Interior monologs,
stream of consciousness, dialogs, and straight-forward
narration are used to aid the reader in his perception
of the different characters. During the novelistic
sequence, Ricardo meets a tragic end, shot while on
maneuvers, Alberto ends up preparing to lead a
"normal" life, and Jaguar marries Teresa and finds
work at a bank. In the end, even the unpredictable
Jaguar, who has been so elusive throughout, finds
his place in society. Let us consider first of all
the psychological implications of determinism.

The underlying psychological basis of La ciudad
y los perros is Freudian. Freud, being a rationalist
and a materialist, was also a great admirer of Darwin,
from whom he derived most of his evolutionary and
biological approaches to the human condition. Therefore many of Freud's theories are related to both the
nineteenth century and to present day concepts of
determinism. However, he went beyond Darwin to arrive
at the belief that man is influenced greatly by
psychological factors and not just by social and
not just by social and material conditions.

According to Freud's theories of psychology:

> There were, it was postulated, two
> great vital drives--the drive for
> self preservation and the drive

toward procreation (i.e., the preservation
of the species). The former presented
no great difficulty to the individual
since it was not ordinarily thwarted
for any prolonged period of time. The
latter, however, to which Freud gave
the name libido or sexual energy, was
frequently blocked from overt expression
by the repressing forces of civilization.[6]

Both the channeling of sexual energy and the desire
for self preservation are prominent factors which
determine, to a large extent, human relations in
La ciudad y los perros.

        The first year cadets are put in a situation
where they have to survive the various hazings, beatings,
and abuses of the older students. Later they are
 aught how to outwit each other and the officials. The
underlying attitude in the Leoncio Prado is that if
the cadets can survive in this environment, society
at large will not be an obstacle for them. For most
of the cadets self preservation is not a problem after
they have learned the rules of the game, but for the
weaker ones, as in the case of Ricardo, this becomes
a tremendous dilemma. To Jaguar self preservation
becomes life's biggest challenge.

        Compounded with the basic adolescent sexual drives
is the idea of machismo which is imposed upon the
cadets by parents, society, and peers. The result is
a preoccupation with sex, manhood, and self-esteem
which at times confuses the individual's ability to
act rationally. Most of the cadets' preoccupations
with sex as described by Vargas Llosa are spectacular:
the masturbation contests, the sodomy, and the
prostitute Pies Dorados, to cite a few examples. Sex
as related to machismo pervades the novel and exercises
a strong psychological influence upon characters. In
the sexual contests between cadets and the constant
desire to know Woman, thus becoming a Man, the author
presents one of the basic motivating forces in male
adolescence. In an interview, Vargas Llosa remarks:

            Uno de esos temas de la novela sería
            la aparición de la sexualidad, que es
            un elemento que ha sido esquivado
            generalmente por nosotros, por nuestros
            autores. El despertar de la sexualidad

no tiene un carácter particularmente
excepcional, es un hecho perfectamente
natural en el proceso de la vida humana,
y dar un testimonio literario de esto,
creo, puede haber producido esa falsa
impresión. . . . El descubrimiento
del sexo puede producir una especie de
conmoción en el hombre, porque la realidad se ensancha notablemente para él,
las inhibiciones vuelan en pedazos,
aparece una nueva dimensión, y eso es
naturalmente violento aunque, por otra
parte, es absolutamente natural.[7]

In La ciudad y los perros the characters are
forced to recognize the importance of sex in their
psychological make-up as individuals. Alberto has the
model of his father to emulate. He is a dandy and
tries to impress upon Alberto the need to become a man
in sexual terms. Combined with peer group pressure
this need becomes an obsession with Alberto, as shown
in his thoughts of Pies Dorados:

Alberto era uno de los que más hablaba
de la Pies Dorados en la sección. Nadie
sospechaba que sólo conocía de oídas
el Jirón Huatica y sus contornos porque
él multiplicaba las anécdotas e inventaba
toda clase de historias. Pero ello no
lograba desalojar cierto desagrado íntimo
de su espíritu; mientras más aventuras
sexuales describía ante sus compañeros,
que reían o se metían la mano al bol-
sillo sin escrúpulos, más intensa era
la certidumbre de que nunca estaría
en un lecho con una mujer, salvo en
sueños, y entonces se deprimía y se
juraba que la próxima salida iría
a Huatica, aunque tuviese que robar
veinte soles, aunque le contagiaran
una sífilis.[8]

Alberto lies about his sexual activities as do
most of the other cadets. He is able to exploit their
sexual fantasies with his imaginative discourses and
production of pornography. But the thought of not
being able to function as a man depresses Alberto and
causes him to think of desperate methods to achieve
his goal. Driven by the urge to exert himself, he is
not concerned about negative consequences. He does

not hesitate to betray his friend Ricardo For Teresa.
While Ricardo is confined, he asks Alberto to deliver
a message to Teresa, whom he has only met on one occasion. Alberto delivers the message, takes her to the
movies, lies to Arana on his return, refuses to write
letters for him and claims Teresa as his own. Ricardo
is not aware of this, of course.

Enroute to Teresa's house Alberto, realizing that
Ricardo is no longer confined at school, imagines the
following scene between Teresa and Ricardo:

> "El entró, le dijo hola, con su sonrisa
> de cobarde, ella le dijo hola y siéntate,
> la bruja salió y comenzó a hablar y le
> dijo señor y se fue a la calle y los
> dejó solos y él le dijo he venido
> por, para, figúrate que, te das cuenta,
> te mandé decir con, ah, Alberto, sí, me
> llevó al cine, pero nada más y le escribí,
> ah, yo estoy loco por ti, y se besaron,
> están besándose, estarán besándose, Dios
> mío haz que estén besándose cuando llegue,
> en la boca, que estén calatos, Dios mío."
> (p. 135)

A look at the above paragraphy reveals that Alberto
imagines Ricardo playing the same role which he had
hoped to fill. His perception of Ricardo's actions
extend even to Ricardo's manner of speech, which is
characterized by uncertainty. The anxiety which
Alberto feels is reflected in manipulation of the verb
besar, "y se besaron, están besándose, estarán besándose, Dios mío haz que estén besándose cuando lle-
gue. . ." This bit of tension on the part of Alberto
proves to be an overreaction, however, as Ricardo,
ironically, never goes to Teresa's after his ill-earned
freedom.

In the treatment of Alberto, Vargas Llosa employs
the stream of consciousness technique to probe the
forces which psychologically determine his actions.
Alberto's fears and his hostilities toward Ricardo
are revealed in this significant look into his mind.
Also, his guilt about having betrayed Ricardo is beginning to surface.

In the case of Ricardo Arana we can see how the
psychological pressures of sex and machismo lead to
his destruction. Ricardo has been pampered through
most of his life by his mother and aunt. There is a

61

"guerra invisible," an invisible war, between Ricardo and his father who confronts him at age ten:

> --¿Eres un hombre? Responde.
> --Sí--balbuceó.
> --Fuera de la cama, entonces--dijo la voz--. Sólo las mujeres se pasan el día echadas, porque son ociosas y tienen derecho a serlo, para eso son mujeres. Te han criado como a una mujerzuela. Pero yo te haré un hombre. (p. 150)

At an early age the idea of manhood is imposed upon Ricardo, who has had the misfortune of being raised in an all feminine environment. There are strong Oedipus Complex overtones in this relationship, as seen in the attachment to his mother and the hate he harbors for his father. After numerous conflicts the father insists that Ricardo enter the Leoncio Prado and become a man.

Once in the institution Ricardo is constantly harassed by the other cadets, who consider him effeminate. This abuse contributes to his finally betraying the entire group. Ricardo's thoughts and fantasies about Teresa make it unbearable for him to remain confined. He tells Alberto:

> --Yo no soy como tú--dijo el Esclavo, con humildad--. No tengo carácter. Quisiera no acordarme de esa chica y sin embargo no hago otra cosa que pensar en ella. Si el próximo sábado no salgo, creo que me volveré loco. Dime, ¿te hizo preguntas sobre mí? (p. 105)

Ricardo subsequently commits a defiant act of survival by divulging the cadet's secrets in exchange for a few moments with Teresa. He realizes that he is losing the important battle of self preservation.

Ricardo is rebelling against the others partly because of the negative image he has of himself, his desire to be a man, and the desperate necessity to be understood. Ricardo discerns that he has failed to learn the basic rules of survival, as revealed in his comparison with Jaguar and Alberto. Ricardo uses Teresa as a pretext to gain his freedom. After he leaves for home, the reader does not receive first-hand knowledge from or about him again until he is shot.

62

Sex, manhood, and self-esteem are the major preoccupations of Ricardo during his brief existence.
Although on the surface he appears to be less affected
by these factors, he does show a quiet determination
to be respected by his peers. Ricardo takes pride in
being second only to Boa in the climax of their contests and he does feel the need to show that he is
capable of a normal relationship with Teresa. His
crucial mistake in this relationship is trusting Alberto, who has the same basic probles as he does, but
will resort to any method to resolve them. The two
basic psychological determinants which form the basis
of La ciudad y los perros, the drives for self preservation and to some extent, procreation, converge on
the character of Ricardo Arana in a way which makes
life unbearable for him. Unable to define himself in
manly or sexual terms, Ricardo, representing the weak,
is eliminated.

While Jaguar shares the same preoccupations with
growing up as the others, his life before entering the
Leoncio Prado is more complete. Having been introduced
to sex and prostitution by Flaco Higueras, his attitude
is much more realistic. This attitude is a result
of the hardships which Jaguar has been faced with
throughout his life. Survival and honor seem to be his
basic priorities. Early in life he has developed a
fierce honor code which he adheres to, unchangingly,
throughout the novel. It is he who solidifies the
Círculo which protects the perros from harassment and
provides illegal means of beating the system. Since
his days of robbing houses with Flaco Higueras, he
knows that the worst crime one can commit is to be a
soplón or betrayer.

Given his sense of pride and his disgust for weakness it follows logically that Jaguar would be the one
who avenges Cava, ex-member of the Circle, by eliminating the weak Ricardo. This, for Jaguar, is an essential part of his conception of masculinity. Self preservation has been ingrained into Jaguar's perception
of the world. His entire psychological make-up is
based on experiences where, since childhood, a hostile
environment has forced him to develop his own method
of confronting the world in a fight for the survival
of the fittest.

Sex to Jaguar is, at times, another tool to be
used for survival as shown in his relationship with his
godmother whom he manipulates for material comfort. As

63

seen in La ciudad y los perros the sexual aspect of
human existence, along with the need for self preservation, goes far in influencing human actions, emotions
and relations. This is evidenced by the psychological
make-up of the characters as revealed in their subsequent acts.

One element of what Rosa Boldori calls determinismo ambiental is the lack of social mobility among
Vargas Llosa's characters. Social stratification is
evident throughout La ciudad y los perros. Vallano
represents the black ethnic group, Cava the serranos,
Teresa the lower class, to add a few more to the already mentioned list. Dislike for different social
groups is shown by the class conscious cadets themselves who apparently learn this at an early age.
Alberto despises anybody below him socially, expecially
Blacks and serranos. He equates love and beauty with
money and class status, as shown in his assessments
of Teresa, Marcela and Helena. Alberto, as part of
his adaptation, finds Marcela and Helena more compatible because of their upper class values.

In Vargas Llosa's novels there is seldom a kind
word, either spoken or implied, for certain social
groups. A negative image of the Afro-Peruvian seems
to be always portrayed. But this is the way it is in
Peruvian society. In Sociología del Perú, under the
"Separación definitiva del negro", Aníbal Ismodes
Cairo asserts, referring to the values prevalent in
Peruvian society:

> Con esto indicamos que los negros, como
> grupo y como individuos, no tienen la
> menor oportunidad para llegar a situ-
> aciones sociales en los que se mueven
> los privilegiados.

While Vallano is not the supreme example of this phenomenon, attitudes toward him reflect certain preconceived notions of where he should fit. This problem will be explored in depth in Conversación en La
Catedral which allows more room for interpretation.
Carlos Delgado notes:

> En el Perú los prejuicios raciales gra-
> vitan en mayor o menor grado, sobre todos
> los planos de la vida social. El "blanco"
> el de "buena presencia" y, mejor aun,
> el extranjero "gringo" tiene una evidente

                ventaja sobre el indio y el mestizo
                para progresar social y económicamente.10

Ismodes Cairo and Delgado are both aware of aspects of
Peruvian social reality such as racism and mobility
which are harshly dramatized by Vargas llosa's fictional personages.   Therefore, there is a great deal of
compatibility between sociological and artistic perceptions of the problem.   Each character is presented
with his stereotypes and popular beliefs surrounding
him intact.

Alberto, with his middle class upbringing, cannot
commit himself to Teresa because of her poverty-strick-
en condition.   It is perfectly all right, however, to
use her as an ego booster and as an instrument of betrayal.   Among his old companions he is at ease playing
the role of successful favorite son.

Jaguar, on the other hand, professes an infantile
love for Teresa which lasts through adolescence and
into adulthood.   He can identity with her situation
of a broken home and poverty because he is faced with
the same situation of struggling for survival.   It is
not surprising that at the end of the novel Alberto
is ready to head for the United States and Jaguar
and Teresa are married.   Although there is interaction
on various social levels in La ciudad y los perros,
the end result is that the status quo is maintained.
Since most of the other cadets are also class conscious
it is assumed that they will each return to their fam-
ilies and carry out their assignments in life, based
more or less on the preconceived notions about class
and society which they demonstrate upon arrival at
school.

The Leoncio Prado represents a microcosm of Peruvian society in which the values and mores are shown
to influence individual actions and decisions.   Attitudes learned on the outside are shown to be at work
within the school.   Alberto sums up the basic attitude
toward life when Ricardo tells him that he is not
going to be a soldier:

                --Yo tampoco.   Pero aquí eres militar
                aunque no quieras.   Y lo que importa en
                el Ejército es ser bien macho, tener
                unos huevos de acero, ¿comprendes?   O
                comes o te comen, no hay más remedio.
                A mí no me gusta que me coman.   (p. 23)

65

Alberto recognizes early that a large part of life involves staying ahead of the other fellow. The cadets have been placed in the Leoncio Prado because they need to become men and how to become manipulative in their relationships with others. Their elders recognize that a period or initiation is needed before they will be able to adjust meaningfully to society. At the end of their terms the primary process of initiation should be complete.

Alberto's thoughts upon returning home are highly significant:

> Su habitación estaba a oscuras; de espaldas en el lecho, Alberto soñaba sin cerrar los ojos. Habían bastado apenas unos segundos para que el mundo que abandonó le abriera sus puertas y lo recibiera otra vez en su seno sin tomarle cuentas, como si el lugar que ocupaba entre ellos le hubiera sido celosamente guardado durante esos tres años. Había recuperado su porvenir. (p. 333)

Symbolically, Alberto is being welcomed to the real world like a long lost son. The reaction of Alberto and the other characters in general to their environment is not over-simplified; rather their final outcome is logical in this closed society which the author represents to us. Angel Rama, referring to the process which takes place in the Leoncio Prado writes:

> Allí, en la soledad, dentro de la circunstancia brutal y sucia, como quien dice dentro de un ahogante protoplasma sangriento, se opera el tantas veces definido como segundo nacimiento: allí nace el hombre por vez definitiva.[11]

The cadets have been defined in social terms by the educational process. The Leoncio Prado has therefore fulfilled its function, which is one of conditioning. Activities within the school have determined what role each youngster will fulfill in the society.

The case of Lieutenant Gamboa will serve to demonstrate how Vargas Llosa sees the political process (defined in the broadest terms), this time manifesting

itself in the form of the military, as thwarting
individual freedom. Gamboa is an upstart officer
who tries to correct what he believes to be wrongdoing
but becomes a victim of the chain of command. After
Arana is shot and killed and the Establishment
dismisses the incident as an accident, Alberto accuses
Jaguar of the crime. Gamboa, who is convinced that
Alberto is telling the truth, attempts to conduct
an investigation against the wishes of his captain,
major, and colonel. As a result Gamboa is transferred
to the wastelands of Puno.

Although he is a good soldier Gamboa discovers
that influences are more important than records or
past performances. He has been up against a stacked
deck from the beginning. Truth and justice are shown
to be of little importance to those who control the
destinies of men. A life is of little significance
when the system is threatened. On paper Arana's
death remains an accident because with the signing
of a paper Gamboa can be sent into exile. Directly
related to Gamboa's case is the fact that the Colonel
blackmails Alberto into keeping his mouth shut, using
the threat of exposing his pornography as a weapon.
Political maneuvering and manipulation seem to be the
order of the day as Vargas Llosa sees it, both inside
the Leoncio Prado and within society at large.

As revealed in La ciudad y los perros, society
and institutions are structured as to impose inhibiting
circumstances upon individuals. Jean Franco observes
astutely that:

> The determinism which many critics refer
> to when speaking of these novels is
> therefore something far more complex
> than the nineteenth century understanding
> of this term. In Mario Vargas Llosa's
> institutions, the organic and the
> structural, the evolutionary process
> and the synchronic relationships are
> antithetical.[12]

The organic and the evolutionary processes which
represent nineteenth century determinism are juxtapositioned in Vargas Llosa's literary world with the
structural and the synchronic relationships of modern
day institutions. Determinism, then, becomes not just
a matter of instinctual drives and desires but rather
a network of factors--individual, social, cultural,

psychological, economic, and political--which shape
human destinies. The result is a picture of frustrated individuals who are constantly at war with their
circumstances.

Jorge Lafforgue has written an article entitled,
"La ciudad y los perros, novela moral", which addresses
itself to the book's moral conceptual basis.[13] Lafforgue's study has very little to do with the explicit
moral questions raised in the novel. Foremost among
these questions is the resolution of the problem of
Jaguar's guilt and punishment. Different opinions have
been expressed concerning whether Jaguar shot Ricardo.
All evidence points in his direction and he confesses
in the end.

In one of the truly dramatic moments of the novel
Jaguar confesses to Gamboa and begs him unsuccessfully
to put him in jail. After being ostracized by his
peers and confirming his belief that they have no conception of what fortitude is, Jaguar decides to make
an example of himself even though, or perhaps because,
he still believes in the rightness of his actions.
Gamboa thinks that the killing of Arana and subsequent
complications have taught Jaguar a moral lesson, as
shown in their final conversation:

> --¿Sabe usted lo que son los objetivos
> inútiles?--dijo Gamboa y el Jaguar
> murmuró: ¿Cómo dice?--Fíjese, cuando un
> enemigo está sin armas y se ha rendido,
> un combatiente responsable no puede
> disparar sobre él. No sólo por razones
> morales, sino también militares; por
> economía. Ni en la guerra debe haber
> muertos inútiles. Usted me entiende,
> vaya al Colegio y trate en el futuro
> de que la muerte del cadete Arana sirva
> para algo. (p. 326)

Gamboa's speech has a twofold effect. First of
all it places the weight of guilt for murder on Jaguar's
shoulders. Ricardo Arana, as a person, was without
the means to defend himself. His was surely a worthless
death which will forever be on Jaguar's conscience. Now
he is defenseless and at the mercy of Gamboa. Secondly,
this occasion gives Gamboa a type of gratification in
knowing that he was right in believing that Jaguar was
guilty. This makes the burden of his exile somewhat
lighter, while at the same time highlighting the reader's

sense of the irony involved.

The hypothesis of "soft determinism" stated at the beginning of this chapter seems to be justified here. Since man is free, he is held morally responsible for his actions. Important aspects of the moral structure of La ciudad y los perros evolves around the culpability of Jaguar and the acceptance of his guilt. He is held responsible for the murder of Arana even though the system will not allow him to be punished. This, as Vargas Llosa sees it, is due to built-in inefficiency. Jaguar also seems to have learned that honor is acceptable on an individual basis but does not have much meaning in society at large, as exemplified in his failure to communicate with the cadets.

Gamboa's lesson, that to follow a code for its own sake instead of applying it with discretion, does seem to have taken effect because when we last see Jaguar he is married and gainfully employed, his past behind him. As the book closes, Flaco Higueras, Jaguar's ex-mentor who is just out of jail tells him: "Pero no podremos vernos con frecuencia, tú te has vuelto un hombre serio y no me junto con hombres serios" (p. 343). In this case "serio" means responsible, as the Leoncio Prado experience has apparently had a positive effect on Jaguar.

Lafforgue's interpretation of La ciudad y los perros does not effectively bridge the gap between determinism, which he implies, and moral responsibility. His final assessment is:

> Un mundo de almas incomunicadas, de destinos prefijados. Personajes que se deslizan sobre la Tierra como los caracteres de la tragedia griega--apenas si el suspenso nos distrae del inexorable fin sabido desde un comienzo. Esto es lo decisivo: un mundo sin porvenir, o con un porvenir abortado de antemano. (p. 239)

Lafforgue's presentation and understanding of the world view of the novel is that of a hard determinist or fatalist. However, there is not enough evidence to support his conclusion or those of the other critics. The case of Jaguar proves that nothing could be farther from the truth. One would expect him to end up as Flaco Higueras if his destiny were indeed predetermined. Rather Jaguar finally emerges as an

69

autonomous individual as a result of his finally com-
ing to grips with the system, but on his own terms.
Gamboa does not make him confess: Jaguar makes his
own choice just as he does when he remains silent
even though he knows that Alberto is the soplón.

We are able to arrive at such a conclusion only
after a close examination of the factors which make
individuals react as they do. Taking into considera-
tion the psychological, social, environmental, political, and moral factors at work, it is possible to see
that characters are indeed highly influenced by outside forces beyond their control but which are imposed
upon them by man, rather than some alien presence.
Their failure has its basis in human activities. The
novel in its complexity shows that there is individual
response to given situations.

LA CASA VERDE

La casa verde offers penetrating insights into
how the environment, society, the political system,
and human behavior help to condition and determine
the outcome of individual destinies. The trajectories
of Liturna, Bonifacia, and Reátegui will serve as illus-
trated examples. The two poles of the novel, Santa
María de Nieva in the jungle and Piura in the desert,
represent two climatically different locales, both of
which are hostile to human existence.

A brief description of physical aspects of each
location, followed by a discussion of the character
Fushía, will reveal some of the environmental obstacles
faced by individuals in their daily activities. In
the opening scene of La casa verde, as the troops move
through the jungle, we observe them:

> Ovillados bajo el pamacari, desnudos de
> la cintura para arriba, los guardias duer-
> men abrigados por el verdoso, amarillento
> sol del mediodía: la cabeza del Chi-
> quito yace sobre el vientre del Pesado,
> el Rubio transpira a chorros, el Oscuro
> gruñe con la boca abierta. Una sombrilla
> de jejenes escolta la lancha, entre los
> cuerpos evolucionan mariposas, avispas,
> moscas gordas.[14]

The scene presented here is one of languor as
humans take the midday siesta coverd by the greenish

70

yellowish sun, reflective of the physical condition
of the jungle setting itself. What we have is a
rather deceptive coexistence between man and nature,
as the pesky smaller creatures let man know that he
is an intruder. As the novel progresses open hostility will rage between man and nature in the Marañón
environs.

The initial description of Piura is also rather
depressing:

> Al cruzar la región de los médanos,
> el viento que baja de la Cordillera se
> caldea y endurece: armado de arena,
> sigue el curso del río y cuando llega
> a la ciudad se divisa entre el cielo y
> la tierra como una delumbrante coraza.
> Allí vacía sus entrañas: todos los días
> del año, a la hora del crepúsculo, una
> lluvia seca y fina como polvillo de ma-
> dera, que sólo cesa al alba, cae sobre
> las plazas, los tejados, las torres, los
> campanarios, los balcones y los árboles,
> y pavimenta de blanco las calles de
> Piura. (p. 31)

Personification of natural forces intensifies
the depiction of this scene. The sands come armed and
impenetrable and apparently perform a daily act of
vengeance upon the city of Piura. In this particular
situation townspeople have tailored their daily lives
to correspond to the dictates of nature. Thus in
both jungle and desert experiences the physical environment represents a formidable opponent to be reckoned
with.

The story of Fushía can be approached from various
angles; as the epic of the frustrated anti-hero who
is prisoner of his existential anguish or as the chron-
icle of a man completely overshelmed by his environment. The apparent contradiction in Fushía shows
both the physical and psychological aspects of his
dilemma as a human being. He is faced with both internal and external problems in confronting reality.

Fushía's movement, because of the unlawful nature
of his work, is limited almost exclusively to the jungle region. He perpetuates a war against his surroundings which eventually devours him. As we first encounter Fushía in the text his lament is to the effect that

71

he does not want to be worthless. His main complaint with life is: "Esa fue mi mala suerte siempre tener que partir de cero" (p. 50). Obviously in a terminal situation, his efforts have not been as rewarding as he had planned.

Early in the narrative, Fushía questions his position in the universe, implying that forces beyond his control have played a role in his final destiny. Others have lost dignity, family, and wealth during the interactions portrayed in the novel but Fushía is in the process of losing his entire sense of being:

> --Y ya ves, todo por gusto--dijo
> Fushía--. Me he sacrificado más
> que cualquiera, nadie ha arriesgado
> tanto como yo, viejo. ¿Es justo
> que acabe así, Aquilino?
> --Son cosas de Dios, Fushía--dijo
> Aquilino--. A nosotros no nos toca
> juzgar eso. (pp. 52-53)

Aquilino takes a stoic approach to Fushía's fate, placing the blame with Dios. On a more immediate level however, a close examination of the evidence will reveal that the environment, his conception of himself, and his relationship to others will expalin more about the cause of anguish than mere speculation about functions of the unknown.

Fushía's life is recounted to us as he makes the trip downriver from his island to the leper colony of San Pablo. Chronologically the voyage is encased within a time period of a month but in terms of human and psychological time it embraces a lifetime of suffering and defeat. Through the use of multiple parallel dialogs we are able to reconstruct events of Fushía's life, from his escape from prison in Campo Grande to his involvement with Reátegui in the illegal rubber traffic with the Axis powers during the war. The latter offense leads to Fushía's exile and he takes Lalita with him as a matter of revenge on Reátegui. However, they never leave Peru, just as Reátegui had planned. He remains in the background manipulating the strings of their destiny.

The technique of elaborating separate parallel scenes within a given verbal structure serve to present past and present simultaneously, thereby immobilizing

time, and highlighting significant events in Fushía's
life. Chronology of occurrence is dispensed with as
important moments in his trajectory pass before him.
This technique is consistent with the author's idea
of presenting the multifacted features of reality.
Fushía is a prisoner of both past (in a psychological
sense), and present (in his physical predicament).
The utilization of multiple parallel dialogs helps to
underscore this determinist aspect of his existence.

While Fushía's most pressing problem is the physical aspects of his present dilemma, many of his past
activities are brought before him. Fushía, along with
the reader, is made aware of the fact that it is not
only the present which is important in his life, but
also the past, which is responsible for the present
and the future. Thus we have a summation of the
forces which were instrumental in structuring this
predicament. The complexities of Fushía's past are
channeled into brief moments of consciousness. This
results in a single reality being presented.

During the entire trip Fushía reiterates his
belief that some force beyond his control is determining the outcome of his life. During the process of
the trip to the leper colony with Aquilino the reader
discovers that nature has indeed played a cruel trick
on Fushía. He has been deprived of his sexual potency,
which is a terrific blow to his ego and concept of
manhood, and the disease which he has makes him detes-
table in the eyes of his fellow man. Fushía is slowly
being eliminated by the natural process. He compares
himself to one of the lower forms of animal life which
appears to have an advantage over him.

Fushía is able to blame his failure with women on
the ladies themselves but his larger problem is far
beyond his comprehension. His life long assumption
is that nature has been unfair to him. However, more
immediate pressure and frustration are caused to
Fushía by the elements which he encounters during his
years of operating in the Marañón region. The early
jungle experience which Fushía relates as he and Lalita flee toward their Indian allies is one of hostility:

> Los escoltaban jejenes, lluvias de zan-
> cudos, el canto ronco de los trompeteros
> y en las noches, a pesar del fuego y
> de las mantas, los murciélagos planeaban
> sobre sus cuerpos y mordían en lugares

                    blandos: los dedos del pie, la nariz,
                    la base del cráneo. (pp. 216-17)

In this immense green house man is far from king, rather
he is at the mercy of the elements. Here the hostile
forces of nature attempt to overwhelm him and destroy
his existence. The onslaught against man is continous,
requiring that he constantly be on guard.

     Perhaps the most agonizing part of Fushía's entire
experience is that he has to watch himself being
eaten away by the disease. Before his illness he had
been able to coexist with his environment but as his
condition worsens, Fushía recognizes the ominousness
of the surrounding forces. His long fight for survival ends as the overpowering natural environment
is brought to the fore. As Aquilino leaves Fushía for
the last time:

                    Murmurar y va retrocediendo, ya está
                    en el sendero. Hay charcas en los des-
                    niveles y un aliento vegetal muy fuerte
                    invade la atmósfera, un olor a savias,
                    resinas y plantas germinando. Un vapor
                    tibio, ralo aún, asciende en capas ondu-
                    lantes. El viejo sigue retrocediendo,
                    el montoncito de carne viva y sangrienta
                    está inmóvil a lo lejos, desaparece
                    tras los helechos. Aquilino da media
                    vuelta corre hacia las cabañas, Fushía,
                    vendría el próximo año, susurrando, que
                    no se pusiera triste. Ahora, llueve a
                    cántaros. (p. 390)

     With this personification of nature, "un aliento
vegetal", Fushía is shown to be completely engulfed by
forces which have been hostile to man throughout the
novel. The scene here is a forceful one as most of
the senses are stimulated. The environment is one of
fertilization as the vaporousness of the setting totally surrounds the protagonist. Fushía's final de-
composition is the last step in his brief, losing confrontation with nature. He is depicted, ironically, as
having a negative union with the universe. Both Fushía
and Anselmo, as shown earlier, triumph momentarily but
yield to greater forces. In Piura and Santa María,
this apparent portrayal of man's constant inability to
cope with nature is dramatized, a fact which ultimately
structures his final negative outcome in two geographical extremes of Perú.

In terms of socialization, the jungle experience
and Bonifacia's process of acculturation are two of
the major themes which are closely bound together in
La casa verde. In this regard the figures of Jum,
Bonifacia, and Julio Reátegui are virtually inseparable.
The effects of society upon the Indian girls are
brought out very early in the novel in a conversation
between Julio Reátegui and the Mother Superior as he
seeks a servant girl:

> El sabía de donde venían estas niñas,
> como vivían antes de entrar a la Misión,
> Julio Reátegui le aseguraba, Madre, había
> habido un error, no lo había comprendido,
> y después de estar aquí las niñas no
> tenían donde ir, los caseríos indígenas
> no se estaban quietos, pero aun sipu-
> dieran localizar a las familias las niñas
> ya no se acostumbrarían, ¿Cómo iban a
> vivir desnudas de nuevo?, la Superiora
> hace un ademán amable, ¿a adorar ser-
> pientes?, pero su sonrisa es glacial,
> ¿a comerse los piojos? (p. 117)

This verbal exchange paradoxically reflects the
situation of the Indian girls. While the Mother
Superior is saving their souls, she is deculturizing
them in the process. This inevitable creates an identity crisis as the girls are trapped between two cultures, and in their "civilized" state both cultures
will eventually despise them. Homeless and stripped
of their heritage, Bonifacia and other Mission products have no other alternative than to go to the
highest bidder.

Julio Reátegui and his wife have, in the past,
"helped" these girls with their "problems" and the
Mother Superior reacts negatively to his request:

> La idea era que ellos ayudaran a las
> madres a incorporar al mundo civili-
> zado a esas niñas don Julio, que les
> facilitaran el ingreso a la sociedad.
> Era precisamente en ese sentido que el
> señor Reátegui, Madre, ¿acaso ella no
> lo conocía? Y en la Misión recogían
> a esas criaturas y las educaban para
> ganar unas almas a Dios, no para propor-
> cionar criadas a las familias, don Julio,
> que le disculpara la franqueza. (p. 117)

The conversation here is strikingly ironic. The
Mother Superior is unbelievably far removed from the
reality of the situation. She has good intentions
but employs the wrong methods. Her primary objective
reverses itself once the girls are beyond the Mission's
walls. Their souls may have been saved but their function in society has been greatly limited. In La casa
verde Bonifacia is the prime example of what becomes
of these newly "civilized" Indian girls.

At the end of their meeting with the Mother
Superior, Julio and don Fabio have their pick of the
girls who are present and Bonifacia, whom Julio had
brought to the Mission earlier is one of his choices.
However, she makes a scene and does not leave, rather,
they take a girl identified as "la de los diente lima-
dos". Clearly there is a conflict between the two
cultures regarding the meaning of civilization. Later,
in an act of rebellion, Bonifacia frees the girls and
is expelled from the Mission for her actions.

Bonifacia's history is dispersed throughout
the novel and told from different angles and points of
view by people separated in time and space. Her fate
after freeing the pupils is related to us before we
know the circumstances in a conversation between
Adrian Nieves and the sergeant. After being expelled
from the Mission Bonifacia is aided by Nieves and Lalita. Eventually she marries the sergeant who takes
her to Piura.

After Lituma kills Seminario in the game of Russian roulette and is sent to prison in Lima, the reality of her situation is impressed upon Bonifacia by
Josefino, her pimp, as they discuss her pregnancy. He
points out to Bonifacia that there is no place in her
life for a child. Pertinent questions posed by Josefino reveal that Bonifacia really does not have a choice
in the matter. Her dilemma is compounded by the fact
that nobody is going to hire a pregnant woman as
housekeeper, which is her last resort. An abortion
and prostitution are her only avenues of survival.
Thereafter as a prostitute, she constantly responds
to the wishes of others. Bonifacia's final assessment of herself is a "puta" and a "recogida". She
has arrived at this station in life through institu-
tional exploitation by the church, the military and the
brothel.

During her lifespan Bonifacia has always been at
the disposal of others, never having much to say about

76

her own destiny. Society and its institutions have persistently manipulated this powerless figure. Basically innocent, she is no match for the whims of the corrupt world, since knowledge gained in the Mission is useless. While Bonifacia is far from being a noble savage, most of her values and beliefs are shown to be subordinated to the exploitative process.

Julio Reátegui, who represents the forces of historical and political determinism, appears in the rubber incident with Jum. Reátegui's subsequent actions set off a chain of events which determine the trajectory of various lives in La casa verde. Outsiders have taught Jum's people to form a cooperative to sell rubber direct to buyers, thus eliminating the middle man, Pedro Escribano, who cheats them. As a result, the Indians have become militant in their efforts to ward off the oppressors. This situation is not acceptable to Julio Reátegui whose duty it is to control the flow of rubber and the Indian lives if necessary. He is also concerned with determining the entire phytogeographical make-up of the region by making rubber a strictly Amazonian enterprise under his control. In the past Englishmen took rubber from the region and began to produce it at a cheaper rate. Reátegui has apparently learned a lesson from history and is determined not to let it be repeated. He intends to keep a tight reign on the Indians and their resources by employing any means necessary.

In La casa verde Julio Reátegui is shown to take an active and important part in determining the character's destinies. His function is rather obvious instead of being "desde la invisibilidad" as some critics maintain. Reátegui's wishes are made quite explicit to Jum:

> . . . el Aguaruna no podía vender
> en Iquitos, que tenía que cumplir sus
> compromisos, que ésos que vinieron los
> habían engañado, que nada de coopera-
> tivas ni de cojudeces. Patrón Excabino
> volvería y que haría comercio como
> siempre traduciendo eso pero el intérprete
> muy rápido señor, repitiendo mejor-
> cito y el capitán te habló despacio nada
> de bromas. (p. 165)

Jum resists Reátegui's extortion attempt and is made an example of for the rest of the Indians. He is crucified and tortured, never regaining the command and respect of his people. The little girl who accompanies Jum--whom we are later able to identify as Bonifacia--is taken away by Reátegui and given to the Mission. This is perhaps the most important event of her life also. Reátegui, as lawgiver, has plans for Jum and "la chiquilla": ". . . castigo por faltar a la autoridad, nunca más pegarle a un soldado, nunca engañando patrón Escabino, sino volverían y castigo sería peor" (p. 185); ". . . las monjitas serían muy buenas, iban a cuidarla mucho, también la señora Reátegui la cuidaría mucho" (p. 187). The author uses the complex technique of narrated monologs to convey Reátegui's belligerent attitude toward his victims.

As Bonifacia passes through the hands of the Church, the military, and finally society at large she is a picture of complete frustration. This is true also for Jum who never regains respectability. Their experiences are linked with the Indian experience of the region as we witness a symbolical first meeting of the two cultures. On one level Julio and the Madre Superiora are reenacting aspects of the Conquest as they discuss Jum and Bonifacia's fate:

> Que tratara de hacerlos entrar en razón,
> aquí le obedecían todos, que no hicieran
> eso con el desdichado. Iba a decepcion-
> arla, Madre, lo sentía mucho pero él
> también pensaba que era la única man-
> era. ¿Otras armas? ¿Las de los
> misioneros, Madre? ¿Cuántos siglos
> estaban aquí? ¿Cuánto se había avan-
> zado con esas armas? (pp. 380-81)

In this dialog the age old question of what to do with the Indian is being discussed as Reátegui favors the more aggressive military solution and the Mother Superior maintains the traditional Church approach. It is ironic that both have the same aim, to deculturize the native and shape him in the mold of the conqueror, either spiritually or militarily. Reátegui, in assuming the posture of lawgiver does not believe in the soft approach to the Indian "problem". As a conqueror he sees force as the only means possible. In the jungle environment of La casa verde, Reátegui and his political machine influence the outcome directly and indirectly of more people than any other single factor.

Jum's life trajectory is also determined by his contact with Reátegui. After losing the leadership

and esteem of his tribe he finally joins Fushía's band
of raiders but never gives up efforts to regain what
has been stolen from him by the soldiers. Fushía and
Aquilino discuss his actions:

> --¿Iba a reclamarles a las guardias
> mientras trabajaba conmigo?--dijo Fushía--.
> ¿No se daba cuenta? Pudo fregarnos a
> todos ese bruto, viejo.
> --Más bien di cosa de loco--dijo Aqui-
> lino--. Seguir con lo mismo después
> de tantos años. Se estará muriendo y no
> se le habrá quitado de la cabeza lo
> que le pasó. No he conocido ningún
> pagano tan terco como Jum, Fushía.
> (p. 317)

At the risk of betraying Fushía, Jum continues the futile quest to recapture his dignity. The psychological burden of his failure as leader follows Jum to
the grave. The rubber symbolizes his manhood which
he is never able to recapture after being humiliated
and made an example of by Julio and his organization.
Jum's amazing capacity for "terquedad", for sticking
to a personal purpose, is not completely snuffed out
however as he continues to fight against the odds.

Jum cannot return to his own tribe because of
his chagrin, nor can he assimilate into another because
of cultural differences. His only choice is to continue the quest, determined to a large extent by Reátegui's
political maneuvering and by Jum's conception of justice. Jum's position is presented succinctly by Aquilino. "Se estará muriend y no se le habrá quitado de
la cabeza lo que le pasó." Emasculation for political
reasons by Reátegui has left an imprint on Jum's mentality which determines his subsequent acts throughout
La casa verde.

In its complexity La casa verde embraces decades
of human experiences. One prevailing trait of characters analyzed is the constant striving to choose the
correct option. At times, this exercising of choice
is thwarted by society, politics, and environment as
we see in the cases of Bonifacia, Jum, Nieves, and
Fushía. A deculturized Bonifacia and an emasculated
Jum are direct results of the political activities of
Reátegui. However, individual choice was exercised by
both, as Bonifacia freed the girls and Jum chose not
to deal with Escabino. Fushía made a rash of unwise

As related to the concept of "soft determinism",
time as a structural element is important in presenting
the reality of a given situation. Often, in La casa
verde, we see the result of an action and the simultaneous process of its development. Causality and predictability are therefore implicit in the presentation
of circumstances which are, for the most part, tragic.

CONVERSACION EN LA CATEDRAL

In Conversación en La Catedral the individual
finds that the political process is geared to thwart
his efforts and to shape his destiny. Just as Santiago Zavala discovers that even in the University
it is not safe to play politics, Trinidad López learns
the same lesson in a more brutal way. Odría's rise
to power in Peru was characterized by his overt efforts
at liquidating the aprista movement. This was probably
one of his strongest campaign pledges. The forms
and motives of this persecution, along with a comment
on the function of APRA, are present in Conversación
en La Catedral where Trinidad López exemplifies one
aspect of this movement. Another dimension of the
political situation is apparent in the presentations of
Trifulcio and Ambrosio.

The lives of Trinidad and Amalia Cerda are bound
closely together as they have a romantic love affair
early in the novel. Trinidad works in a textile fac-
tory near the laboratory where Amalia goes after she
is fired from the Zavala household. In the novel Trinidad's relationship to APRA is presented in an ambiguous manner.

Trinidad claims to have come from a proletarian
background in Pacasmayo where he has been jailed for
aprista activities in the past. Amalia, being politically naive, is curious about the activities of Trinidad:

> ¿Trinidad era aprista?, y él hasta la
> muerte, ¿y había estado preso?, y él sí,
> para que veas la confianza que te tengo.
> Se había hecho aprist hacía diez años, le
> contó, porque en ese garaje de Trujillo
> todos estaban en el partido, y le
> explicó Victor Raúl Haya de la Torre
> es un sabio y el Apra el partido de los
> pobres y cholos del Perú.[15]

Trinidad appears to be an activist who is aware of

80

the political reality of his time. He has allegedly experienced persecution under Bustamante and now Odría. But serious doubts are raised concerning the validity of Trinidad's assertions because of the postures assumed by different narrators. This is all a part of the author's narrative strategy in the attempt to capture an event in its totality. In and out of jail as waht could be called a political fanatic, Trinidad's activities with Pedro Flores, cohort, lead to a final arrest and death. The fact that the police do not know whether Trinidad is an activist is insignificant since their duty is to wipe out the opposition. The final irrational act of Trinidad is related to Amalia by Pedro Flores:

> Y le contó: volvían de una fieste-
> cita en Barranco y al pasar por la Emba-
> jada de Colombia Trinidad para un ratito,
> tengo que bajar, Pedro Flores creyó que
> iba a orinar, pero bajó del taxi y co-
> menzó a gritar amarillos, vival el Apra,
> Víctor Raúl, y cuando él arrancó asus-
> tado vio que a Trinidad le llovían ca-
> chacos.
>
> ....
>
> . . . Y mientras Amalia lloraba a la
> señora Rosario le contaron que lo habían
> encontrado esa madrugada en la puerta del
> Hospital, que se había muerto de derrame
> cerebral. (I, p. 104)

Trinidad assumes the posture of an aprista although he supposedly had no political affiliation. He does not really understand the deeper implications of the movement although he is beaten and tortured several times and finally killed. Amalia experiences a double tragedy because she loses here baby several days after Trinidad dies and is left alone to suffer.

Regardless of Pedro Flores' version of Trinidad's life history, there is always the possibility that Trinidad was telling the truth about his political background and activities. The fact remains that he was persecuted and killed. Ambrosio and Santiago are instrumental in recapturing some of the circumstances surrounding Trinidad's activities.

Due to flagrant persecution of the apristas most sane individuals would have denied having political

81

contact with Trinidad as does Flores. On the other
hand, both Santiago's account of Trinidad's imprisonment,
through Fermín's actions, and Trinidad's version
correspond. Flores' contention that he is Trinidad's
cousin is contradicted by the latter.

Vargas Llosa presents the Trinidad López experience
from several different angles which are separated in
time and space. The situation itself is very ambiguous
and critics have offered varying opinions concerning
Trinidad's functions. Oviedo writes:

> No nos extrañe pues, que nunca se aclare
> del todo quién es realmente el obrero
> Trinidad Fernández (sic), si es un
> excéntrico que se hace pasar por
> aprista o si es en efecto un militante
> que se disimula (I, 104), si muere a
> golpes o si él va por su cuenta
> al hospital (I, 106).[16]

The mystery concerning Trinidad's appearance at
the hospital door is cleared up by Ludovico and
Hipólito in their conversation with Lozano. After
beating and troturing him until he is unconscious
and unable to function they leave Trinidad: "--En
la puerta del San Juan de Dios, señor Lozano--dijo
Hipólito--. Nadie nos vio" (I, p. 186). Lozano
refuses to cooperate with his henchmen after they have
applied too much pressure and they are faced with
disposing of Trinidad themselves.

Vargas Llosa describes the last moments experienced
by Trinidad in chapter nine as he is being interrogated
by Ludovico and Hipólito. Under the pressure of
questioning, Trinidad who appears to be an unstable
individual suffers a mental breakdown. While he is
being torutred, Trinidad apparently acts out his
fantasies about APRA and his delusions of grandeur.
He is hoping for a revolution by APRA which does
not come.

Trinidad's ordeal is interspersed with sketches
of dialogs from different points in time but which
are thematically related. On one level Trifulcio is
performing his function as bodyguard for Arévalo.
Juxtapositioned is the discussion between Cayo and
Fermín concerning La Musa and homosexuality as
related to the political situation of the country.

82

Hipólito who has homosexual tendencies himself, physically and sexually exploits Trinidad as he tortures him.

While Vargas Llosa is presenting the persecution and suffering of the APRA, he appears also to be making a critical comment about vital aspects of the movement. The only character who actively identifies with the aprista movement is Trinidad López who is shown to be a political fanatic without any true commitment. He is a great chanter of slogans but the depth of his knowledge is questionable. Consequently he dies a frustrated death. In Conversación en La Catedral both the apristas and the Odría regime are presented in a negative light as they try to nullify each other. Victims of this political process are the naive Amalia and Trinidad who do not understand the functions of their institutions, but nevertheless, whose lives are determined, in the final analysis by these very institutions.

In the novels of Mario Vargas Llosa ethnic groups such as the Indian, the Oriental and the Negro do not fare well as the author treats this aspect of Peruvian social reality. These groups are either relegated to obscure social roles as in the case of the Orientals or their final result is total frustration which is revealed in the Indian and black experiences. Vargas Llosa has expressed his attitude toward the Indian problem in Peru and has written critical introductions and appraisals of indigenista works but oddly enough Indians appear in his works without any real positive values. Examples of these are the primitive cultures, sharpas, huambisas and aguarunas, presented in La casa verde and seen as only a step advanced beyond the Stone Age, waiting to be exploited at will by the strongest.

In Conversación en La Catedral two of the primary characters in the structure of the work are zambos, Ambrosio and his father Trifulcio. This particular mixture of Indian and Negro carries an implicit tension which is externalized in the novel. Political and social determinism, as related to mobility, is an essential part of the analysis of these characters.

Early in the narrative we discover that they are from Chincha and are accustomed to a life of hard times. Trifulcio's literary birth is surrounded by negative animal images as Ambrosio relates how he remembers seeing him only once in his entire life. Trifulcio is criminally inclined and in jail. We are presented the interior of the prison from the viewpoint of a "gallinazo," or buzzard, as the men below are at the mercy of the elements. There is inherent violence in the scene as the bird of prey devours an iguana:

> Dulcemente el ave rapaz aleteó a ras
> de tierra, la trapó con el pico, la
> elevó, la ejecutó mientras escalaba
> el aire, metodicamente la devoró sin
> dejar de ascender por el limpio,
> caluroso cielo del verano, los ojos
> cerrados por dardos amarillos que el
> sol mandaba a su encuentro. (I, p. 130)

Violence and destruction are the order of the day as this bird rises majestically above the scene. But the buzzard is in turn trapped by the prisoners and devoured. The basic concern here is for survival.

This scene is made more complex and intense by the three different levels of reality which are being presented. First, there is the position of Trifulcio who appears to be wishing for some type of salvation: "--Ojo que ahí viene--dijo Trifulcio--. Ojo que ahí baja" (I, p. 130). Trifulcio is obviously hoping that the bird comes down near him but at the same time he is wishing for liberation, which arrives in the form of don Melquiades and Emilio Arévalo.

On another level the "ave rapaz" image is related to the activities of Cayo Bermúdez who has ordered troops to occupy the University of San Marcos while Coronel Espina was in the north. The implications of other political activities surrounding Trifulcio at this point are extremely significant. For politics, more so than any other factor, will chart his life's trajectory.

Ambrosio who is analogous to the "ave rapaz" as destroyer in the dog pound, represents a third point of view as he relates to Santiago and don Fermín, in separate conversations, the relationship between himself and his father whom he scarcely knew. His final impression of him is: "--Un moreno canoso y enorme que caminaba como un mono--dijo Ambrosio--. Quería saber si había mujeres en Chincha, me sacó plata.

No tengo buen recuerdo de él, don" (I, p. 131). We
are presented with a dehumanized vision of Trifulcio
from the beginning as the elements and society are
shown to be at work against him.

Ambrosio's main complaint against Trifulcio is
the painfulness he feels because of the lack of
dignity and respect for himself and others on Trifulcio's part. He is a very repulsive sight but in the
prison where Trifulcio was confined, conditions for
survival are such that human beings are just above
the existence level. At any rate, Trifulcio is
released from prison for political purposes, to serve
in the senatorial campaign of Emilio Arévalo. As
Trifulcio raises the keg to display his strength
Arévalo calls him "un verdadero toro." A sense of joy
and exhilaration surrounds Trifulcio as he leaves the
prison, so great is this freedom but he is not a free
man since he belongs to Arévalo.

In Conversación en La Catedral Trifulcio is
characterized as an instrument who is powerless to
do anything except what others demand of him. This
has apparently been the case throughout life because
he is already at an advanced age when the novel opens
and appears to be accustomed to the role he plays.
"El que daba las órdenes" is the prevailing motif in
Trifulcio's mind as he works for Arévalo as bodyguard.

The demonstration in Arequipa which leads to his
death is approached cautiously by Trifulcio. He knows
that the altitude has an adverse effect on him and
that he is suffering from soroche. Trifulcio is
humanized somewhat in the end; his last thoughts are
of Chincha as he is kicked to death: "Aire, como un
pescado, Tomasa, atinó todavía a pensar" (II, p. 144).
Trifulcio appears on the scene as a sub-human animal,
lives, and dies as one. He is buried in an unmarked
grave as somebody who passed through life without
ever having a chance to live it. The political process
has completed its use and destruction of Trifulcio.
Like Trinidad he is shown to be powerless but Trifulcio
is literally led to his fatal ending by the whims
of politicians.

Ambrosio's case is much more complex than that of
his father since his subjective view of events is
paramount to the narrative. As presented, socio-
political forces which account for a lack of social
mobility are foremost in his ultimate outcome. We

first encounter Ambrosio when Santiago goes to rescue
his dog. Ambrosio has worked as an interprovincial
chauffeur and came to Lima with apsirations of being
somebody. Instead, he works for Bermúdez and Zavala
as chauffeur and is forced to go to Pucallpa after
allegedly killing Hortensia who is blackmailing Zavala
because of homosexual relations with Ambrosio. After
his wife, Amalia, dies Ambrosio leaves his daughter,
Amalita Hortensia, with a neighbor, steals a bus and
returns to Lima. Although he is degraded and dehumanized throughout life, Ambrosio does have certain
positive qualities. But as revealed in his battle for
survival, he cannot escape the dilemma of being an
underdog in society. An innocent Ambrosio leaves
Chincha with aspirations, but on arriving to Lima he
quickly discovers that the only way to survive is by
adapting to the corrupt system, which entails a loss
of humanity. This process of dehumanization is
related to the fact that Ambrosio, as an individual,
cannot win the big battles of life because of factors
beyond his control.

Conversación en La Catedral in its ethnic
dimension shows, among other things, the inability of
Ambrosio to break the social-political-economic bonds
which shackle him. The assertion that Ambrosio lacks
will is an error. Evaluations of the character of
Ambrosio generally coincide with the conclusion of
José Miguel Oviedo who states that, ". . . la vida ha
anulado en él toda rebeldía y toda conmoción interior."[17] The novel is basically concerned with how
society succeeds in shaping the individual, sometimes
in perverse ways. Life's processes have degraded
Ambrosio almost to the level of the animals which he
is killing. However, beneath a superficial reading
of the text one can see that Ambrosio represents more
than just a loyal and docile servant. His mentality
is not completely slave oriented and he does have a
positive image of himself. When Queta calls him Cayo
Bermúdez's servant, Ambrosio retorts: "No soy sirvien-
te de nadie--dijo el sambo, tranquilo--. Sólo soy su
chofer" (II, p. 208). During the interactions with
Queta, which are narrated throughout the novel, an
apparently insignificant act such as working months
to earn enough money to purchase her favors is nonethe-
less important to Ambrosio's ego. He considers this a
positive act because Queta operates in the upper crust
of society.

Another very important aspect of social determinism in the portrayal of Ambrosio is his lack of social mobility. In opposition to him is Ludovico, strongarm man, bodyguard, and demonstration breaker whose principal ambition is to be put on the escalafón, that is, to be admitted into the system of corruption because of his brutal political activities. This idea becomes an obsession with him. Ludovico and Ambrosio work together on numerous occasions and their trajectories are in close parallel. We see Ambrosio functioning only as chauffeur. Ludovico becomes a police official and Ambrosio a dog pound worker.

Here Vargas Llosa is using this contrast to show the difference in the life's chances of the two individuals and the advantage of being smiled upon by the corrupt political system. Frankly, there is no place for Ambrosio to go but down. Later we learn that in order for Ambrosio to go into exile in Pucallpa, ironically, he has to bribe his old friend Ludovico.

As presented in Conversación en La Catedral, options open to Trifulcio and Ambrosio are very limited. The former has spent most of his life as a bodyguard and Ambrosio is a chauffeur. Santiago offers him a job as doorman which is better than working in the pound. At any rate, the positions of Trifulcio and Ambrosio in the novel, although they represent extremes, appear to be compatible with the overall social status of Afro Peruvians in general. Their position in society appears to be marginal at best and since they do not have any resources the most they can hope for is to exist. Society has already defined for them what they can and cannot do. In Vargas Llosa's presentation it appears to be impossible to break the never ending chain which keeps them submerged in mediocrity. This is amplified by the fact that they are living in an era of corruption.

There has been a lot of ink spent on the ethnic situation in Peru and undoubtedly there is much more to be written. In light of situations and characters presented in Vargas Llosa an examination of certain attitudes will help to illuminate important aspects of his interpretation of Peruvian social reality. Sociological studies usually treat the mestizo-cholo-Indian problem and place little emphasis on the black situation. Fernando Fuenzalida Vollmar who tries to make sense of the ethnic reality of Peru in his article,

"Poder, etnia y estratificación social" writes: "Son tres los criterios que definen la raza social de una persona, con hincapié distinto según la región en que se apliquen: ascendientes, apariencia física y status sociocultural."[18] Ambrosio and Trifulcio strike out in all three counts, becoming social non-entities. Their background is insignificant, their physical appearance repulsive, according to accepted norms which stress whiteness, and they lack sociocultural status.

In presenting this human drama to us Vargas Llosa is obviously aware of the social ramifications of the situation of Ambrosio and Trifulcio. From the first moment they are seen and described, a different dimension is added to the story. Whether the problem is biological or cultural, as normally maintained when discussing Peru, the end result is the same. The fact that Ambrosio is a black zambo does have a lot to do with his inability to succeed in society. R.J. Owens writes:

> A white skin or Spanish descent is a great social advantage, though there is no absolute bar on mixed blood. Negroes, however, have little chance of social advancement, nor are the yellow races much welcomed; but an admixture of Negro or oriental blood is tolerated provided the physical characteristics are not too pronounced.[19]

Aníbal Ismodes Cairo states:

> No hay un solo miembro del grupo negro que pueda tener la ocasión de franquear esa barrera social levantada por la clase privilegiada y en la cual se amuralla definiti- vamente. El negro es el gran segregado social. Rara vez como individuo llega al campo profesio- nal donde se desenvuelve la clase media. Nunca a la clase alta.[20]

The manner in which Vargas Llosa, the artist, conveys the experiences of individual characters is much more rewarding, in spite of the author's negative portrayals, than sociological documentation. We are able to live moments with society's outcasts by observing the interpersonal relationships between characters which are transmitted through dialogs, thoughts, suppositions and remembrances. Attitudes of characters are of the utmost importance in presenting aspects of social reality. The negative reaction of Santiago's mother to his mestiza wife is ethnically motivated along with Fermín's opinion of Cayo Bermúdez's cholo background. As reflected in Conversación en La Catedral, the lowest as well as the highest echelon of society seem to be aware of these inherent racist attitudes in the social composition of Peru. In many instances, attitudes in conjunction with institutions help determine the outcome of individual destinies.

In La ciudad y los perros, La casa verde, and Conversación en La Catedral Vargas Llosa presents to us the effects of political, psychological, social, and environmental forces on human lives during given periods of Peruvian history. Lives are intermingled and frustrated as these forces continue to shape the individual, thwarting his attempts at advancement. This is more pronounced among less fortunate elements of society as revealed in the novels. Images of defeat and degradation amplify the sense of entrapment which characters feel and experience as they struggle to come to grips with forces which govern them.

The concept of soft determinism elaborated at the beginning of the chapter holds true. The characters studied in La ciudad y los perros, La casa verde, and Conversación en La Catedral are affected by causality and predictable circumstances but their freedom to choose, albeit from limited options, is not denied. The degree of pessimism expressed in the world views of these novels is as much an indication of the author's disenchantment with Peruvian society as his character's capacity for failure.

Existentialism

As interpreted today, the philosophical doctrines of determinism and existentialism are not necessarily opposed to each other, that is, if we accept the categories of "hard" and "soft" determinists as most critics do. The idea of soft determinism embodies what may be called an "existential determinist" viewpoint which does not deny man's freedom to choose but which, at the same time, recognizes that certain forces will shape him.

In treating problems of the philosophical underpinnings of Vargas Llosa's novels, several critics
have discussed the opposition of determinism and
existentialism. Harss and Dohmann write, in a very
unclear way, "Vargas Llosa seems to fluctuate between
old-fashioned determinism--which leaves room for free
choice--and Sartrean situationalism, a difficult
concept to embody dramatically."[21] George McMurray
observes: "Perhaps due to Vargas Llosa's political
convictions and interest in contemporary French
literature, his novels reveal a mixture of two totally
different philosophies: social determinism and
existentialism."[22] Since both determinism and
existentialism are definite factors in Vargas Llosa's
world view, it is also necessary to explore aspects
of existentialism and its importance in character
portrayal.

In the literary world of Mario Vargas Llosa many
different factors influence individual destinies but
the right to choose is never denied his characters.
True, choices may be limited but each individual is
faced with the problem of defining himself. He must
not merely exist; rather the challenge is to make life
meaningful, which often leads to a certain realization
of inadequacy and to conflict with self and surroundings.

Although existentialism as a description of the
human condition has probably been with us since man
began to contemplate his relationship to the cosmos, it
is generally agreed that this philosophical doctrine
received its official name from, and gained popularity
at the beginning of the twentieth century with, Søren
Kierkegaard. Existentialism rapidly became the doctrine
which was used by writers and philosophers to describe
their outlook on life.

Existentialism as expounded by such thinkers as
Gabriel Marcel, Karl Jaspers, Martin Heidegger and
Jean Paul Sartre adopts the position that in defining
himself, man is forever searching for ways to combat
alienation, search for his essence, and achieve
authenticity in existence. The search itself seems
to be of utmost importance, even if it is of a
Sisyphean nature. From the existentialist's viewpoint
there is a certain dignity attributable to man's
constant striving, even if it is against a hostile
universe which offers no encouragement.

Jean Paul Sartre, perhaps, has influenced most modern writers more than any other existentialist thinker because of the way in which he systematized and expounded ideas concerning this philosophy. Many critics have commented on Vargas Llosa's predilection for Sartre,[23] and there are numerous parallels which can be drawn. These range from existentialism to his concept of the function of literature.

Existentialism is one of the major philosophical and literary preoccupations of the twentieth century. The following brief, standard summary will prove useful in this exploration of the doctrine:

> The existentialist's point of departure
> is the immediate sense of awareness
> that man has of his situation. A part
> of this awareness is the sense man has
> of meaninglessness in the outer world;
> this meaninglessness produces in him a
> discomfort, an anxiety, a loneliness
> in the face of man's limitations and a
> desire to invest experience with
> meaning by acting upon the world,
> although efforts to act in a meaning-
> less "absurd" world lead to anguish,
> greater loneliness and despair.[24]

The formulation of the existentialist doctrine itself evolved from man's striving to live and act in the chaotic, tragic, and confusing new world. In spite of this pessimistic view of the human condition Sartre asserts that, ". . . what we can say from the very beginning is that by existentialism we mean a doctrine which makes human life possible. . . ."[25] Possible, yes, but at times miserable. Sartrean terminology will therefore be used to interpret Vargas Llosa's existential attitude toward the human condition in Conversación en La Catedral.

According to Sartre, each individual has the obligation to make something of his life on earth by shaping and choosing his own destiny. It is a human responsibility to exercise the will and judgment to this end. Therefore existence (just being here) precedes essence (the real matter of life), an attitude which is the exact opposite of how philosophers traditionally viewed the process of self definition.

Although at this early stage in his literary
career it would be presumptuous to try to formulate
a definitive statement about Vargas Llosa's overall
world view, one of the basic philosophical underpinnings
of his literary works is existentialism. As previously
stated he attempts to reconcile determinism and
existentialism. An analysis in depth of one character
will shed light on the presence of existential thought
in his work. Obviously, the implications are extendable,
although not identically, to other characters.

CONVERSACION EN LA CATEDRAL

Santiago Zavala, along with Cayo Bermúdez and
Ambrosio Pardo, is one of the leading characters in
Conversación en La Catedral. A great deal of the
action is narrated and discussed from his point of
view. What the reader receives many times is a
subjectivization of his apparent objectivity; therefore,
what he is leaving out may be as important as what he
is telling. This holds true for Ambrosio also, as
both he and Santiago reconstruct this crucial period
in their lives and in Peruvian history.

Santiago himself provides the basis for an
existential interpretation because he is pictured as
being the disillusioned intellectual and self-
disinherited son of the bourgeoisie, who is determined
to relate to society on his own terms. His efforts to
find some essence in life are thwarted by factors
which he had not taken into account and he slowly sinks
into despair and cynicism, unable to comprehend his
position in the world.

A close character analysis will show the process
by which Santiago is tranformed from the favorite son
to an aspiring communist, and finally to a newspaper
columnist in a dead-end job in the newspaper La Crónica.
Conversación en La Catedral begins with the epilog (we
discover as the novel progresses), as Santiago
contemplates the city of Lima and relates it to his
personal destiny: "El era como el Perú, Zavalita, se
había jodido en algún momento. Piensa: ¿en cuál?"
(I, p. 13). Zavala's preoccupation throughout the
novel will be how both country and individual have been
betrayed by the same forces, which he believes to be
principally of a political nature.

The incident which sets the novel in motion occurs
when Santiago goes home for lunch and finds that his

dog, el Batuque, has been taken from Ana, his wife, and
is now in the pound. The Depósito Municipal de Perros
is described by Santiago as, "Un gran canchón rodeado
de un muro ruin de adobes caca--el color de Lima,
piensa, el color del Perú--. . . ." (I, p. 19).
With this nauseating description Santiago continues to
manifest his hostility toward, and lack of respect for,
the situation of his country by relating it to negative
images of filth and degradation. In the dog pound he
meets Ambrosio, ex-chauffeur for his father whom he
has not seen for twelve years. As they enter the
restaurant from where the text of the novel will ema-
nate, Santiago suddenly undergoes a series of guilt
feelings.

An accusative voice of consciousness addresses
Santiago and implores that he not enter the conversation with Ambrosio because of the psychological dis-
comfort it will cause him. As they drink and talk,
thoughts of his father continously recur, overshadow-
ing the hustle and bustle of the dirty atmosphere of
La Catedral: ". . . ni tú ni yo teníamos razón papá,
es el olor de la derrota papá" (I, p. 27). This confessional, defeatist attitude permeates the novel.

Conversación en La Catedral is encased within a
chronological time period of approximately four hours
although it accounts for lifetimes of psychological
and human experiences. Santiago's guilt feelings are
aroused and as they prepare to leave he offers Ambrosio
the job of doorman in La Crónica and a month's salary
which Ambrosio contemptuously turns down.

Anxious and guilt ridden, Santiago returns home
realizing that he has spent more money than he should
have and the chapter ends with another negative image
of Lima. In this first chapter Vargas Llosa presents
a Santiago who is definitely searching for meaning in
his existence. Money, alcohol, and marriage--major
preoccupations of modern man--are also problems for
him. These observations are conveyed to the reader
by the thoughts, descriptions, and conversations of
the actors in this drama of life.

In the narrative structure of the work, questions
posed to Santiago by Ambrosio in Chapter 1 are answered
in Chapter 2. In this retrospective chapter we have
the first indications of Santiago's rebellion against
his parents and religious elements as he expresses
his political and religious views. Santiago is determined to go to San Marcos rather than to the Catholic

University and he has already developed an anti-Odría
attitude. At the same time he is developing a sense
of right and wrong as shown in his desire to give his
allowance to Amalia, the servant, who has been fired
because of her relationship with the boys. Santiago
reconstructs the two incidents, their taking advantage
of her and his giving her money, simultaneously through
the use of parallel dialogs.

As he prepares to enter San Marcos, Santiago has
some fundamental questions which he must ask himself
concerning his political and personal function in the
university:

> ¿Cómo se podía ser comunista sin saber
> siquiera si existía un partido comunista
> en el Perú? A lo mejor Odría los
> había encarcelado a todos, a lo mejor
> deportado o asesinado. Pero si apro-
> baba el oral y entraba a San Marcos,
> Aída averiguaría en la Universidad,
> se pondría en contacto con los que
> quedaban y estudiaría marxismo y se
> inscribiría en el Partido. (I, p. 76)

One of Santiago's main ambitions is to become a Communist. He finds help in Aída, veteran of the student
movement, but at the same time falls in love with her.
This results in a triangular relationship with Jacobo,
self-styled leader and revolutionary whom Santiago
uses as a personal sounding board in his search for
identity: "Otro puro de ésas piensa, en rebelión
contra su piel, contra su clase, contra sí mismo, contra el Perú. Piensa: ¿seguirá puro, será feliz?" (I,
p. 83). This alienated view of a person in conflict
with his very existence is an accurate description
of Santiago at this stage of his own development. However, at the same time he is questioning the validity
of this attitude; does alienation from ethnic background, social class, and self necessarily lead to
happiness? This is a fundamental question which Santiago never answers.

As members of the Communist cell Cahuide both
Santiago and Jacobo who are from Miraflores, maintain
the philosophy that the best revolutionaries come from
the bourgeoisie. They break with their class only
superficially. Santiago tries to lead a dual existence by living with his parents and by being against
what they represent at the same time.

Although one of Santiago's pressing childhood fantasies is to become a Communist, he never joins the Communist Party. When the time comes for him to make the decision he backs down, an act which forever haunts him:

> Yo prefiero seguir como simpatizante--el gusanito, el cuchillo, la culebra--. Tengo algunas dudas, me gustaría estudiar un poco más antes de inscribirme. (I, p. 160)

"El gusanito, el cuchillo, la culebra" is a motif which highlights the amount of internal tension being felt by Santiago. The inability to break with his past is pointed out to him by Carlitos and this is borne out by Santiago's actions throughout the novel.

The fact that he cannot lead the same type of existence as Jacabo and Aída forever haunts Santiago. They are able to make mistakes and rectify them, something he is unable to accomplish. But he is grateful to the San Marcos experience for transforming him from a model student into a dissident:

> --Porque gracias a San Marcos me jodí--dice Santiago--. Y en este país el que no se jode, jode a los demás. (I, p. 160)

This familiar motif in Vargas Llosa reveals that Santiago, as Peruvian man, has two choices--betray his fellow man or himself. He opts for the latter and begins leading a Sisyphean existence while in conflict with self, family, and society.

An important self realization comes for Santiago during a series of clandestine meetins of Cahuide in which they are trying to decide whether to be violent or non-violent in thier support of the striking workers. Santiago's entire effort at being a revolutionary leads to the nauseous conclusion that he does not have the psychological equipment. Of course he is not alone, for this is one of the realities of this particular political posture. In his work on Sartre concerning the "Intellectual as Impossible Hero" Victor Brombert writes, "The political tragedy of their time finds them awake and aware but secretly convinced that they have no mandate whatsoever.[26]

Perhaps the most significant event of his life takes place when Cahuide is broken up by the police and Santiago has to be rescued by his father, don Fermín, who is in turn humiliated by Cayo Bermúdez. Santiago is not allowed to suffer the consequences of his arrest and this subsequently remains a pressing issue on his consciousness. Santiago is never able to regain the respect of his cohorts because of the intervention of Fermín on his behalf.

Book One ends as Santiago leaves home trying desperately to define himself. He begins work in La Crónica, supposedly temporarily. Indeed life does become even more frustrating for Santiago as he is unable to improve either himself or his surrounding. In the process of self definition Santiago becomes alienated from society, country, and self. This is the situation in which we encounter him as the novel begins.

The many forms of alienation, a concept which describes the individual's sense of estrangement, is one of the basic ingredients of existentialism. Different ramifications of this concept are prevalent in Conversación en La Catedral and La casa verde.[27] In his treatment of the topic, G. Petrovic offers a useful summary:

> Twentieth-century writers differ greatly in their enumeration of the basic forms of alienation. Frederick A. Weiss has distinguished three basic forms (self-anesthesia, self-elimination, and self-idealization); Ernest Schachtel has distinguished four (the alienation of men from nature, from their fellow men, from the work of their hands and minds, and from themselves); Melvin Seeman, five (powerlessness, meaninglessness, and self-estrangement); and Lewis Feuer, six (the alienation of class society, of competitive society, of industrial society, of mass society, of race, and/or generations).[28]

Santiago is shown to embody many of these forms as the novel progresses, principally the categories outlined by Schachtel, Seeman, and Feuer.[29]

There are many contradictions in Santiago's

character, basic among which is his attempt to mentally break with his family while physically remaining in Miraflores. This exemplifies his inability to dissassociate himself from his upbringing regardless of his bohemian existence. Thus we are able to reconstruct Santiago's life from adolescence through maturity. His greatest problem is disillusionment with life, which leads to utter despair. He is alienated and in constant disagreement with the social, political, and educational processes of Peru. Santiago feels walled in, isolated, and rejected. He realizes that he is imperfect and unable to carry out his major objectives. As a result he retreats into cynicism, searches for meaning in the world and realizes that human existence is absurd.

In his portrayal of this aspect of Santiago's dilemma, Vargas Llosa coincides with one of Sartre's principal existential themes, the notion of absurdity, or the contention that circumstances have no sufficient reason for being as they are. Santiago's consciousness of absurdity is revealed in the persistent "¿En qué momento se había jodido el Perú?" Santiago finds himself in a senseless world of which he tries to make senese.

Alienation and absurdity are but two of the major existential themes of Vargas Llosa which have been discussed so far in Conversación en La Catedral. They are also prominent in La casa verde, especially in the character of Fushía who, in his final moments, seeks meaning in existence. Two other pressing existential problems of Santiago are freedom and choice, and anxiety and dread. Beginning with the latter, most existentialists, principally Kierkegaard, argued that in certain psychologically defined moments, truths about human nature are grasped when we realize that we do not fear specific objects but experience a generalized dread. In Sartrean terms this fear or anxiety is seen as a confrontation with the fact of freedom, of our unmade future. This is precisely what happens to Santiago when he asks himself: "¿Qué me pasa hoy?" This metaphysical question remains unanswered as he finds himself lost in an incomprehensible world. This is also visible to some extent in Fushía's attitude toward the idea of Aquilino leaving him.

As an existentialist writer, using Santiago Zavala as a model, Vargas Llosa's assessment of the human condition is compatible with current literary interpretations. Man's reaction to reality is one of frustration and alienation, as he stands basically alone, regardless of his surroundings. Efforts to communicate personal thoughts and inner desires are futile and thwarted because of societally influenced barriers to communication and understanding. As man turns inward to self, he sees only tragedy and despair in the universe.

Conversación en La Catedral has been called a novel of complete frustration and this is shown to be true in respect to the outcome of individual destinies. There is an overwhelming air of defeatism, both individual and societal, pervading the novel as it relfects a clearly defined period of Peruvian political, historical and social reality.

The central thesis of most existentialists and especially the early Sartre is that the possibility of choice is the central fact of human nature. Sartre's 'existence precedes essence' states that first of all, man exists, turns up, appears on the scene, and, only afterwards, defines himself.[30] Later he states, "Man is condemned to be free. Condemned, because he did not create himself, yet, in other respects is free; because, once thrown into the world, he is responsible for everything he does."[31]

Santiago Zavala fails miserably in his attempts to define himself. The choices he makes all seem to be of the wrong nature. As a result of these choices he experiences mental anguish, a sense of frustration and anxiety, feels that his existence is absurd and becomes alienated from country, society, and self. Existential hero, "Sartrean" intellectual, disillusioned Peruvian--Santiago is all of these and more. He represents the end product of a social process with which the individual finds himself unable to cope. It is worthwhile to note that Fushía as anti-hero encounters the same situation although his arrival is by a different process.

Vargas Llosa uses technique--principally the stream of consciousness method--and time as a structural element to bridge the apparent contradiction between determinism and existentialism. Through a retrospective simultaneous presentation of events separated in time and space, Vargas Llosa elaborates important mental recollections and associations which impact forcefully upon individual destinies in the past, present, and future.

In the novels of Mario Vargas Llosa lifetimes are encapsulated within hours (Conversación en La Catedral), days (La ciudad y los perros), and months (La casa verde). Time as his characters perceive it is a complex multidimensional experience. By juxtaposing the stream of consciousness technique, usually associated with existentialist writing, with a dynamic conception of time, and by presenting the functions of institutions upon humans, Vargas Llosa is able to literarily reconcile the two seemingly different doctrines of determinism and existentialism.

Both internal and external structure are important in the interweaving of the two doctrines. In the works discussed aspects of existentialism (alienation and its themes, process of self definition, Sisyphean persistence) serve as themes which are effectively developed by a number of technical resources, such as fragmentation of time, space, and point of view. From the determinist angle, it is evident in the novels that nature, instinctual drives, and society's institutions manifest themselves in the lives of characters as hostile and inescapable forces. The cohesiveness of each work is maintained by weaving these diverse elements of human reality into an artistic whole.

NOTES

[1]José Miguel Oviedo, Mario Vargas Llosa: la invención de una realidad (Barcelona: Seix Barral, 1970), p. 96.

[2] Gerald Dworkin, Determinism, Freewill and Moral Responsibility (Englewood Cliffs, N.J.: Prentice Hall, 1970), pp. 3-4.

[3] Edward D'Angelo, The Problem of Freedom and Determinism (Columbia: University of Missouri Press, 1968), p. 1.

[4] Joseph T. Shipley, ed., Dictionary of World Literary Terms (Boston: The Writer, 1970), p. 80.

[5] Rosa Boldori, "La ciudad y los perros, Novela del determinismo ambiental," RPC, No. 9-10 (diciembre 1966), 92-93.

[6] J.A.C. Brown, Freud and the Post-Freudians (Baltimore: Penguin Books, 1966), p. 20.

[7] "Sobre La ciudad y los perros de Mario Vargas Llosa," Casa de Las Américas, Año 5, No. 30 (mayo-junio 1965), 76-77.

[8] Mario Vargas Llosa, La ciudad y los perros (7th ed.; Barcelona: Seix Barral, 1971), pp. 93-94. Cited hereafter in the text.

[9] Aníbal Ismodes Cairo, "Separación definitiva del Negro," Sociología del Perú (2nd ed.; Lima: Rocarme, 1969), p. 101.

[10] Carlos Delgado, Problemas sociales en el Perú contemporáneo (Lima: Campodónico, 1971), p. 69.

[11] Angel Rama, Literatura y sociedad, Año 1 (octubre-diciembre 1965), p. 120.

[12] Jean Franco, Spanish American Literature since Independence (New York: Barnes and Noble, 1973), p. 262.

[13] Jorge Lafforgue, "La ciudad y los perros, novela moral," Nueva Novela Latinoamericana (Buenos Aires: Paidos, 1969), pp. 209-40.

[14] Mario Vargas Llosa, La casa verde (11th ed.; Barcelona: Seix Barral, 1971), p. 9. Cited hereafter in text.

[15] Mario Vargas Llosa, Conversación en La Catedral, 2 vols. (Barcelona: Seix Barral, 1969), I, p. 93. Cited hereafter in text.

[16] Oviedo, p. 237.

[17] Oviedo, p. 197.

[18] Fernando Fuenzalida Vollmar, "Poder, etnia y estratificación social," Perú: hoy (2nd ed.; México: Siglo XXI, 1971), p. 22.

[19] R.J. Owens, Peru (London: Oxford University Press, 1964), p. 72.

[20] Ismodes Cairo, p. 101.

[21] Luis Harss and Barbara Dohmann, Into the Mainstream (New York: Harper & Row, 1967), p. 36.

[22] George McMurray, "The Novels of Mario Vargas Llosa," Modern Language Quarterly, 29, No. 3 (1968), 338.

[23] The reference here is to the early Sartre.

[24] C. Hugh Holman, ed., A Handbook to Literature (New York: Odyssey Press, 1960), p. 193.

[25] Jean Paul Sartre, Existentialism and Human Emotions, trans. Bernard Frechtman (New York: Citadel Press, 1957), p. 10.

[26] Victor Brombert, ed., "Intellectual as Impossible Hero," The Hero in Literature (New York: Fawcett Publications, 1969), p. 263.

[27] Sara Castro Klarén treats this problem in "Fragmentation and Alienation in La casa verde," Modern Language Notes, 87, No. 2 (March 1972), 286-99.

[28] G. Petrovic, Encyclopedia of Philosophy, ed. Paul Edwards, I (New York: MacMillan, 1967), p. 78.

[29] As a side note, it is worth mentioning that Fushía also lends himself to analysis in terms of existentialism as his quest is also presented in the form of a search for meaning. "Powerlessness, meaninglessness, social isolation, normlessness, and self estrangement" as features of alienation are but a few of his major preoccupations.

[30] Sartre, p. 15.

[31] Sartre, p. 23.

CHAPTER 4

HISTORY: THE PERUVIAN DIMENSION

Aspects of Peruvian historical, political, and social reality form the backbone of the major novels of Mario Vargas Llosa. It is Peru, from city to jungle, which is the subject matter of La ciudad y los perros, La casa verde, Conversación en La Catedral and Pantaleón y las visitadoras. In assessing Peruvian history, Vargas Llosa presents the functions of military and political institutions which not only caused historical changes, but which are also responsible for prevailing attitudes. While the author is not concerned with writing a stylized history of Peru, historical figures are often alluded to and the inner functions of a given period are dealt with artistically. His novels are generally set in the forty year period from 1920-1960 and cover regimes from Leguía through Odría.[1]

This study seeks to reveal how Vargas Llosa views and interprets artistically the various periods of Peruvian history. Also the study will demonstrate how historical figures and events are presented and the manner in which idiosyncrasies of the inner workings of society are affected by historical forces. Vargas Llosa, as artist, has a distinct advantage over the historian in attempting to deal with facts. He can recreate aspects of an age, a society and a situation by the use of devices not available to the historian. The historian is limited to arguments based on verifiable evidence, whereas the novelist may particularize, be selective, and take the approach which is more compatible with his method and intentions. Also, in contrast with those historians who claim to maintain balance and proportion, the literary artist is not bound to give a fair statement of all points of view.

In an interview in 1967 Vargas Llosa shows his awareness of the artist's obligation when he interprets and recreates history:

> Desde luego, cuando un escritor se
> propone en un libro mostrar determinado
> aspecto de la vida social o histórico,
> debe exigírsele que sea veraz, que
> si alude a hechos reales lo haga con
> honestidad.[2]

103

"Con honestidad" are key words here and they do not
necessarily mean that an author has to recreate events
as they happened which could result in mere
documentation, but rather that the experience which he
creates should maintain some semblance of verisimili-
tude. Good faith, objectivity, and expressed desires
of people involved are qualities which should be taken
into account when real historical characters are the
subject matter. From Vargas Llosa's viewpoint, the
artist is not supposed to distort as he reshapes events
in a creative manner. Vargas Llosa continues:

> Pero no me engañó, sé muy bien que la
> verdad histórica y social es una cosa
> y otra la verdad literaria. Una novela
> puede ser históricamente irreprochable,
> moralmente irreprochable, sociológicamente
> irreprochable y resultar ilegible.[3]

Here Vargas Llosa alludes to the difference between
document and experience, which is one of the basic
differences between history and literature. The
artist is free to make documentation a part of the
experiences of characters and situations presented,
so there is no clear cut distinction for the writer.
But the work is also "history" in the sense of being
an autonomous creation which reflects aspects of a
particular era.

While discussing the distinction/comparison
between history and literature Amado Alonso makes the
general observation that:

> . . . la historia y la poesía no se
> distinguen necesariamente por la materia
> tratada, pues si la historia se ocupa
> solamente de las cosas sucedidas, la
> poesía se ocupa tanto de las sucedidas
> como de las inventadas; se distinguen
> radicalmente por el modo de tratar la
> materia; la historia se ocupa de las
> cosas acaecidas, en su significación
> particular; la poesía en su significación
> universal. El poeta puede, pues, tomar
> sus temas de la historia, pero a
> condición de que su mente vaya hacia el
> sentido universal de los hechos históricos
> particulares. En suma, al historiador
> le ocupa lo particular con un sentido

particular; el poeta extrae de lo
particular su sustancia ideal.[4]

To Amado Alonso, the basic difference between history
and literature, in artistic terms, lies in the method
of dealing with subject matter. The writer's task is
to particularize the general experience and give it
universal significance while combining fact and
non-fact.

Therefore, the artist is not to be looked upon
as a source of historical documentation: rather, he
provides us with the intrahistoria or vida privada,
the daily occurrences in the lives of a people, at a
given time and place. His literary expression enriches
our understanding of the "truth," in the case of
Vargas Llosa, of Peru and of aspects of Latin America.
This entails his being aware of the social and political
reality of his time. The novelist usually gives his
own interpretation of the actions of a historical
figure or of an event, filling the gaps in the story
according to this interpretation of character and
circumstance.

Vargas Llosa starts with history in the background
as a framework and then molds his literary world along
this basis. The presence of history helps to better our
understanding of the material being interpreted by the
author. Through fiction he presents the state of
mankind during a defined historical age. This chapter
demonstrates how a greater knowledge of the historical
basis of Vargas Llosa's novels can enhance our
appreciation of them as works of art.

LA CASA VERDE

The action of La casa verde takes place during a
particular historical time and place. Although precise
dates are not given, which suggest a reluctance to be
pinned down historically by Vargas Llosa, critics
agree it is between 1920-60.[5] This is made more obvious
by the problematic social nature of the work itself.
Especially during these years there were many conflicts
and much exploitation of the Indians of the Amazon
region in the great quest for rubber. The Leguía
oncenio (1919-1930) is usually singled out as an example
of administrative insensitivity to the atrocities
committed. R.J. Owens remarks: "It was during his

first term in office, indeed, that some of the worst
exploitation of forest Indians by the holders of rubber
concessions on the Putumayo took place."6

Although in La casa verde the exploitation of the
Indian tribes for rubber does not purport to be an
account of the aforementioned atrocities, the smaller
dilemma presented is symptomatic of a larger problem
of the Peruvian jungle reality. Exploitation happens
to be the rule rather than the exception. Therefore,
there is a firm underlying historical basis for the
manner in which the Indian rubber episodes are handled
in the novel.

My primary intention is to explore the literary
significance of Luis M. Sánchez Cerro, mestizo
President (1931-33), in the work, and to arrive at an
understanding of the historical and political forces
and ideas in contention at that moment. The critical
thrust in my treatment of Sánchez Cerro in La casa
verde is twofold. In the first place I will examine
how Vargas Llosa shows that the myth of Sánchez Cerro
was a sustaining one. Secondly, my focus will be
on how Vargas Llosa's understanding of Sánchez Cerro
was different from that of most social scientists
and historians.

In La casa verde concrete allusions to Peruvian
historical reality are made by the inconquistables in
their perception of Sánchez Cerro and his relationship
to the Mangachería, poor and popular barrio of Piura
which receives a great deal of attention in the novel.
As the different locales of the novel are established
in the first chapter, the reader immediately comes in
contact with some extremes of the popular element in
the form of the inconquistables. Much of their activity
takes place near Sánchez Cerro Avenue which apparently
stops at the very beginning of the barrio. This street
is constantly before the reader and becomes a motif of
the Mangachería setting as the novel runs its course.

A street has been named in Sánchez Cerro's honor
but it is situated in ironic juxtaposition to his
followers:

> Con la avenida Sánchez Cerro terminaban
> el asfalto, las fachadas blancas, y los
> sólidos portones y la luz eléctrica, y
> comenzaban los muros de carrizo, los

> techos de paja, latas o cartones,
> el polvo, las moscas, los meandros.[7]

The people who maintained such vivid recollections of
their idol have not participated in the progress and
prosperity which is now associated with his name. The
naming of the street politically symbolizes progress.
But in social terms it is of little help to the
mangaches. Living conditions remain barely tolerable,
although prosperity is only a few steps away.

The comments of Lituma and Mono are significant
as they rehash old times:

> ---Los blancos se han vuelto valientes
> --dijo Lituma--. Ahora se pasean por la
> Mangachería como por su casa.
> --La culpa es de la Avenida--dijo el
> Mono--. Ha sido un verdadero fusilico
> contra los mangaches. Cuando la estaban
> construyendo, el arpista decía nos fre-
> garon, se acabó la independencia, todo
> el mundo vendrá a meter la nariz en el
> barrio. Dicho y hecho, primo. (p. 39)

A tradition is being destroyed as the outside
world invades the barrio, formerly a private mangache
world, in the name of progress. Just as other important elements in the novelistic structure are developed,
such as Anselmo and the green house, Lituma and Bonifacia, to mention a few, motifs and allusions associated with Sánchez Cerro are also prominent in the work.

Among the residents of the Mangachería there is a
sense of solidarity and brotherhood which has been
built up over the years. This point is discussed by
two of the inconquistables when the question of their
pride in the Mangachería arises:

> --¿Por qué están tan orgullosos?
> ¿De qué la alababan tanto?--dijo
> Josefino--. Huele mal y las gentes
> viven como animales. Por lo menos quince
> en cada casucha.
> --Veinte, contando los perros y la
> foto de Sánchez Cerro--dijo el Mono--.
> Esa es otra cosa buena de la Mangachería,
> no hay diferencias. Hombres, perros,
> cabras, todos iguales, todos mangaches.
> (p. 60)

In the author's attempt to develop the theme of Sánchez
Cerro and his importance and relationship to the residents of the Mangachería, Vargas Llosa's overt method
of allusion and suggestion is compatible with the declamatory and boisterous attributes of the characters
themselves. The reader's perception of the presentation of subject matter and character reaction are
therefore closely related.

In an oft-quoted interview with Emir Rodríguez
Monegal concerning the political and historical implications of the Mangachería, the following comments
are attributed to Mario Vargas Llosa:

> Los mangaches son vagabundos, mendigos,
> artistas. Todas las orquestas piuranas,
> todos los conjuntos musicales, salen siempre
> de ahí, de ese grupo humano que es una
> especie de lumpen y es además la única
> fortaleza que tenía el fascismo en el
> Perú. Porque el General Sánchez Cerro,
> que era piurano según la leyenda, aunque
> no es cierto, era una especie de santo de
> la Mangachería. El partido profascista
> que fundó ese general y que hoy día es
> practicamente inexistente ha tenido
> siempre fieles adherentes en ese
> barrio y sólo en ese barrio.[8]

To Vargas Llosa, speaking from his upper middle
class viewpoint, Sánchez Cerro may have been a fascist
but most students of Peruvian history tend to disagree
with him.[9] This period has to be seen within its
socio-politico-historical context. A brief summary
will prove helpful in an interpretation of the importance of Sánchez Cerro in La casa verde. When
Sánchez Cerro assumed leadership by overthrowing
Leguía in 1930, apristas who had been in exile because
of persecution by the previous administration returned
and resumed their political agitation. Their were
many factors which motivated the renewed oppression
against APRA. In Peter Klarén's estimation:

> Uno de ellos fue el alarmante número
> de disturbios que con regularidad estall-
> aban en todo el país y que amenazaban
> la poca estabilidad que había sido
> capaz de establecer el régimen de
> Sánchez Cerro.[10]

Sánchez Cerro resorted to repressive means to restore
order, with APRA as one of his principal targets.
Early in 1931 he resigned and went into voluntary
exile for several months. In the 1931 elections
Sánchez Cerro and his Partido Unión Revolucionario
presented a platform which appealed to the masses and
which the oligarchy reluctantly accepted, thus under-
mining APRA's appeal to the middle sectors. In what
is generally regarded as one of the most honest
elections ever held in Peru, Sánchez Cerro won. Haya
de la Torre immediately called for armed conflict and
months of bloody battle ensued.[11]

Sánchez Cerro's populist appeal was due, among
other things, to the fact that one of his principal
stated objectives was to bring the dispossessed into
the mainstream of Peruvian life. The following
excerpts of political rhetoric, characteristic of
his approach to the problem, are from a speech of
August 22, 1931:

> La defensa de las instituciones
> democráticas y la necesidad de atender
> las justas demandas de las clases pro-
> letarias, constituyen las dos más
> urgentes necesidades de la hora presente.

> Amo al pueblo con gratitud y con
> convicción. Deseo su mejoramiento y
> su bienestar, y aspiro a conseguírlos,
> en forma ampliamente democrática, difun-
> diendo la cultura popular, desarrollando
> y perfeccionando la legislación obrera
> existente, elevando el nivel de la vida
> del proletario y abriéndole oportunidades
> para que pueda llegar hasta donde su
> capacidad lo permita. He aquí la manera
> honrada, justa y eficaz de proteger
> a las clases trabajadoras.[12]

His platform, as far as social issues were concerned,
was very close to the one offered by Mariátegui and
his followers. During this turbulent period in Peruvian history it is difficult to clearly distinguish
between what the different political factions represented. One thing that does emerge, however, is a
picture of Sánchez Cerro as a strong leader with
popular support.

Sánchez Cerro's impact on the Peruvian political

process is still being evaluated by political scientists and historians. Speaking of the criollos in Lima and Sánchez Cerro's ascension to power, Peter Klarén points out:

> Muy pocos de ellos advirtieron que, no
> obstante el corte aparentemente tradicio-
> nal de los sucesos políticos que condu-
> jeron al golpe de agosto, las reglas
> del juego político nunca volverían
> a ser exactamente las mismas, porque
> el desconocido Sánchez Cerro, un mes-
> tizo de origen modesto, al derribar el
> gobierno de Leguía, inauguraba sin
> saberlo, la participación de las masas
> en el proceso político peruano.[13]

What we observe in La casa verde, then, is an overt manifestation of prevailing popular sentiment of the times which is incarnated in the mangache spirit and pronounced verbally by the inconquistables who are portrayed by the author as being fanatics. As the inconquistables take their first drink to celebrate Lituma's homecoming the image of Sánchez Cerro is very prominent: "José encendió la vela de la hornacina y, a su luz, el recorte de periódico mostró la silue-ta amarillenta de un general, una espada, muchas conde-coraciones" (p. 63). The mangache political posture is even more pronounced when one of them remarks later: "Aquí en la Mangachería todos somos urristas--dijo el Mono, poniéndose de pie de un salto--. Fanáticos del general Sánchez Cerro, hasta el fondo del alma" (p. 83). Critics of Vargas Llosa usually do not pay much attention to the political implications of the mangaches and their importance to the novel. Rather the Inconquistables are singled out as social and economic misfits, expressions of false machismo, and of little significance except for plot as related to the development of Lituma. However the Mangachería and its inhabitants assumes a significant ideological importance in the thematic development of the novel. They are products of an unjust socio-economic system which Sánchez Cerro sought to correct and failed.

In his portrayal of the inconquistables and the importance of the legend of Sánchez Cerro to the mangaches Vargas Llosa literarily weaves aspects of Peruvian reality into a fictional projection of important popular values. Standards of living in the Mangachería demand functional myths and modes of escape. Apparently the

inconquistables do represent verbal manifestations of
popular political feelings which were present throughout parts of Peru when they learned that one of them,
meaning the pueblo, had become President. Vargas Llosa
as interpreter of Peruvian myths and legends is well
aware of this importance.

A keen critical attitude toward the Sánchez Cerro
question is demonstrated by José Miguel Oviedo who
describes him as a

> . . . tosco y ultraconservador militarote
> que llegó a ser presidente del Perú. El
> 'urrismo' de los mangaches es sentimental,
> legendario: existía la falsa creencia de
> que el General había nacido en ese barrio,
> que un mangache había sido exaltado a
> la presidencia.[14]

The question surrounding Sánchez Cerro's origin is also
one of the pressing questions in the novel as the
inconquistables are unable to resolve this issue:

> --El año pasado se vino a vivir aquí
> un aprista, Lituma--dijo el Mono--. Uno
> de esos que mataron al General. ¡Me da
> una cólera!
> --En Lima conocí muchos apristas--dijo
> Lituma--. También los tenían encerrados.
> Rajaban de Sánchez Cerro a su gusto, decían
> que fue un tirano. ¿Algo que contarme colega?
> --¿Y tú permitías que rajaran en tu
> delante de ese gran mangache?--dijo José.
> --Piurano, pero no mangache--dijo Jose-
> fino--. Esa es otra de las invenciones de
> ustedes. Seguro que Sánchez Cerro nunca
> pisó este barrio. (p. 83)

In addition to Sánchez Cerro's origin, the problem
of aprista persecution, one of the trademarks of his
regime, is introduced by Lituma who was obviously in
jail during much of this turbulent period. The other
inconquistables were involved, to a lesser extent, in
Piura through their attack on an aprista family. The
precise dates of Lituma's encarceration are unimportant
because the author eliminates historical documentation
and through the power of allusion and suggestion
recreates aspects of the epoch.

Biographers of Sánchez Cerro share the same problems as the mangaches.[15] It is an accepted fact that

he was born in Piura; whether in the Mangachería is
questionable. Nevertheless, he has been converted into
a living legend and the people apparently associate
him with positive values such as bravery and fortitude.
Thus the question of Sánchez Cerro's origin remains
ambiguous and the author raises this fundamental contradiction in his characters' awareness of this aspect
of the political reality of Peru.

But the importance of Sánchez Cerro is also significant to the overall meaning and to one of the basic
themes of La casa verde, the frustration of heroic
intent. This is touched upon by Oviedo when he alludes
to the heroic tradition of the mangaches. For them,
Sánchez Cerro represented a popular leader with heroic
possibilities. He always led a reckless life which
entailed several escapades in jail, aborted revolts,
and finally he led the coup which overthrew Leguía.
Faced with ungovernable circumstances after becoming
President, he was assassinated, an example of the limited possibilities of true heroism. By choosing a
historical figure to do this, particularly Sánchez
Cerro, Vargas Llosa accentuates the plight of the
mangaches themselves as they identify with their hero.

Sánchez Cerro's popularity with the masses can be
attributed to the facts that he was accessible to the
public while in office, sympathized with them, had
charisma, and maintained a certain manly posture: "En
realidad, el más humilde pastor probablement había oído
del macho, del comandante mestizo que se había traído
abajo al una vez poderoso Leguía."16 This is precisely
the attitude set forth by the mangaches who share, to
some extent, the positive attitude toward life shown by
their idol. Socially and economically down and out, the
mangaches, collectively, have to resort to pride and
physical and verbal manifestation of their feelings in
identifying with a man and with an ideal which they
could understand and appreciate.

In La casa verde Vargas Llosa appears to be more
interested in examining periods of Peruvian history than
expressing a concern for precise dates. And as the
author sees it, during the twentites and thirties turmoil was the order of the day in Peru. This is revealed in his portrayal of the nature of the Amazonian
experience and the "urrista" posture assumed by the
mangaches which was a result of political upheaval.
The author is, of course, dealing with particulars of
the overall experience, or with small facets, of an

112

overall historical issue, such as the enmity between Sánchez Cerro and Aprismo. This microscopic focus gives him greater literary freedom but also illuminates the larger historical scene.

Peruvian history provides the background for the enactment of human drama in La casa verde. Characters such as Jum and Bonifacia, and the inconquistables are shown to merely exist within history, which greatly limits their personal options. Man is presented as being inseparably linked to a tragic set of circumstances which are imposed, to a large extent, by the historical setting.

CONVERSACION EN LA CATEDRAL

In the interview cited earlier regarding history and literature, Vargas Llosa states:

> Por ejemplo, ahora estoy escribiendo una novela situada en el Perú entre 1948 y 1956 y, en un afán de documentación, he llegado a la inaudita proeza de leerme los discursos del general Odría, nuestro presidente de entonces.[17]

In Conversación en La Catedral, the novel alluded to, some of the characters and situations portrayed are historically identifiable and this helps to maintain the author's link to history. But as the reviewer in the Times Literary Supplement points out in reference to the overall meaning of Conversación en La Catedral, "It's triumph is to get across to the reader ugly truths that no number of factual news reports could convey."[18] So Vargas Llosa as literary interpreter of Peruvian reality employs fictional devices in a manner which combines fact and non-fact to enrich the total experience of the reader.

As a work of art Conversación en La Catedral combines elements of both the political and historical novels.[19] The era of Odría is the setting with ample political intrigue but the novel clearly sets politics and political actors in a historical frame. It is in his characterizations and portrayal of events that Vargas Llosa approaches the function of a historical novelist. Georg Lukacs observes that:

> What matters therefore in the historical novel is not the retelling of

113

great historical events, but the
poetic awakening of the people who
figured in those events. What matters
is that we should reexperience the social
and human notives which led men to
think, feel and act just as they did
in historical reality.[20]

The artist interprets various causes which
produced the facts by exploring the secrets of the
human heart which are usually neglected by historians.
He demonstrates artistically that historical circumstances and characters existed in a certain way at
a given moment. The writer also familiarizes us with
the peculiar historical qualities of the inner life
of an age by a broad portrayal of its nature of existence, by showing how thoughts, feelings and modes of
behavior grow out of this basis.

Vargas Llosa artistically captures these motives
in the portrayal of both primary and secondary characters in Conversación en La Catedral. An examination of the figure of Cayo Bermúdez, the recreation of
the uprising in Arequipa, along with a brief examination of APRA form the basis of my assessment of the
author's interpretation of the Odría regime.

Conversación en La Catedral is Vargas Llosa's
most ambitious novel and deals with the ochenio of
General Manuel Odría whose cuartelazo overthrew
Bustamente in 1948. Although the novel is about the
political dealings and relations of this period, it
is narrated by two apolitical persons, Santiago Zavala
and Ambrosio Pardo. Chronologically Conversación en
La Catedral lasts four hours but in terms of novelistic
time it encompasses the entire Odría regime, the Prado
Administration, and the beginning of Belaúnde leadership (1948-63). During a chance meeting, Santiago,
ex-bourgeois favorite son, and Ambrosio, ex-chauffer
of Santiago's father, reconstruct via memories, conversations, and suppositions, this critical period in
Peruvian history. They try desperately to resolve,
among other things, the question, raised in the very
first pages of the novel, "En qué momento se había
jodido el Perú."

Corruption is one of the major themes of Vargas
Llosa as he creates the atmosphere surrounding and
permeating the Odría regime. Indeed, he writes in
his assessment of the period.

> Fue una dictadura muy particular la
> del general Odría; menos sanguinaria y
> espectacular que sus contemporáneos
> en América Latina--la de Rojas Pinilla,
> la de Pérez Jiménez, la de Trujillo,
> la de Somoza--, pero compensatoriamente,
> más corrupta. No quiero decir que en el
> "ochenio" no se matara o desterrara,
> sino que, en general, el Gobierno de
> Odría prefirió, como norma, el robo,
> el soborno y el chantaje, a la matanza.
> Pienso que en esos años todo el
> Perú, de un modo u otro, se contaminó de
> la mugre oficial, y que todos los per-
> uanos nos frustramos y envilecimos un
> poco.[21]

If Vargas Llosa did purport to portray the utter frustration and hopelessness of a society during a critical period in its history he was successful; for Conversación en La Catedral expresses a very pessimistic view of the human condition. Individuals, classes, and Peru itself are shown to be one huge conglomeration of defeatism mainly because of the oppressive nature of political corruption and dealings.

One of the principal proponents of the corrupt aspects of the regime is Cayo Bermúdez, Director and later Minister of government. He is historically identifiable with the Peruvian strongman of the period and projects a negative image to this day. César Lévano writes:

> Alejandro Esparza Zañartu (a) Cayo Ber-
> múdez es uno de los personajes cen-
> trales de Conversación en La Catedral,
> la última novela de Mario Vargas
> Llosa. Esparza Zañartu, sabor a saña.
> Personaje que la cólera civil estrelló
> contra el muro de la historia. Nombre
> que miles de peruanos maldijimos durante
> años desde el fondo de las cárceles.[22]

In his novels it appears that Vargas Llosa is using historical figures in at least two different ways. There is direct naming in the case of Sánchez Cerro, and indirect identification of Cayo Bermúdez. Odría himself appears in Conversación en La Catedral only once. Perhaps the author's hesitancy to employ names is partly due to the fact that these men were still alive when the novel was written. Odría, for example, was recently buried.23

Although Cayo Bermúdez is based upon a historical personage, in the novel he achieves his own autonomy of existence by the manner in which he is characterized. The figure of Cayo in itself, as a reproduction of Esparza Zañartu, is not overly important in the novel; rather, the manner in which he functions in the intrahistoria of Peru is significant. Cayo reflects a certain critical attitude which brought about important historical changes.

Before Cayo appears in the novel most of his personal history is presented intact. The Lieutenant has left Lima for Chincha to seek him out for service in government at the request of Espina, the "Serrano", his old friend. Intermingled with the Lieutenant's activities, narrated in third person is Ambrosio's monolog, identifiable by "don", as he fills in the early childhood of his ex-companion. Later in the narrative the reader discovers that Ambrosio is relating this information to Fermín Zavala, at some point in time, during a visit to his hide-away. Ambrosio later explains his access to so much knowledge through hearsay.

Cayo is shown to come from a very humble background. Corresponding to his family's increase in worldly value is a decrease in moral values. Ambrosio relates how he and Cayo ceased to be friends:

> Después los separó el Buitre, don,
> la vida. A don Cayo lo metieron al
> Colegio José Pardo, y a Ambrosio
> y a Perpetuo, la negra, avergonzada por
> lo del Trifulcio, se los llevó a Mala,
> y cuando volvieron a Chincha don Cayo
> era inseparable de uno del José Pardo,
> el Serrano. Ambrosio lo encontraba en
> la calle y ya no le decía tú sino usted.24

El Buitre, Cayo's father, instills in him at an early age the idea of getting ahead. Ambrosio, his former playmate is soon looked upon as his servant. Cayo has a future but it changes drastically after he elopes with Rosa. When he first appears in Conversación en La Catedral Cayo is leading an ordinary existence.

Before assuming the position of Director Cayo

116

already has preconceived critical notions about Peru
and the manner in which it is governed. Enroute he
tells the Lieutenant: "Aquí cambian las personas,
Teniente, nunca las cosas." (I, p. 60) Speaking
of the people and forces which influence the country's
future Cayo remarks to Espina: "Bueno, mientras los
tengan contentos, apoyarán al régimen. Después, se
conseguirán otro general y los sacarán a ustedes. ¿Siempre no ha sido así en el Perú?" (I, p. 68) Cayo comes
to Lima with ideas about vital functions of the country
and its people which are used to support his subsequent aggressive and self serving actions.

Cayo's next move is the ordering of the occupa-
tion of the University of San Marcos without higher
authorization. He is in the process of taking Espina's
job which the latter is quick to realize. Cayo plays
down his personal lust for power and is assigned
the task of finding the origin of a clandestine paper
La Tribuna. This quest is directly related to the
persecution of an unidentified aprista who appears in
the narrative at this particular moment, being tortured
by Hipólito and Ludovico. Cayo has delegated his au-
thority to Lozano who in turn recieves help from his
aides:

> Ahí hay uno de ésos que te gustan,
> Hipólito--dijo Ludovico--. El señor
> Lozano nos lo recomienda especialmente.
>
> --Lima sigue inundada de pasquines
> cladestinos asquerosos--dijo el coro-
> nel Espina--. ¿Qué pasa, Cayo?
>
> --Que quiénes y dónde sacan La
> Tribuna clandestina y en un dos por
> tres--dijo Ludovico--. Mira que tú
> eres de ésos que me gustan.
>
> --Esas hojitas subversivas van a
> desaparecer de inmediato--dijo Bermúdez--.
> ¿Entendido, Lozano? (I, p. 138)

In this passage events are narrated in reverse order
as we first have the on-going effect and then the
cause of events which happens to be Cayo. The torture begins, the problem is stated, and the order is
given. A certain amount of chaos is evident in the
technique employed thereby reflecting the complexity of the situation.

117

One of Cayo's inherent problems is that he
thinks he knows what is best for Peru, more than
anyone else. He attacks with a vengeance everybody
and everything with which he does not agree maintaining
that, "Este no es un país civilizado, sino bárbaro
e ignorante. . . ." (I, p. 139).

Cayo's attempt to control the government takes
him to the archives for matters of national security.
He realizes that the momentary support which the regime
enjoys is subject to change drastically at any time.
Cayo needs evidence with which to neutralize internal
enemies. Cayo shows keen insight into the political
situation and realizes early that the only way to
control his cohorts is on a personal level. The
archives, therefore, hold the key not only to his own
success but to that of Peru also. A look at United
States and Peruvian relations reveals that a semblance
of democracy in the form of fixed elections brings more
monetary credit to the military junta. The naive
American attitude toward the political reality is
harshly dramatized during the preparation for
subsequent 'elections:'

> --Todo es cuestión de empréstitos
> y de créditos--dijo don Fermín--.
> Los Estados Unidos están dispuestos
> a ayudar a un gobierno de orden, por
> eso apoyaron la revolución. Ahora
> quieren elecciones y hay que darles
> gusto.
> --A buscar trabajo allá--dijo Am-
> brosio--. En la capital se gana más.
> --Los gringos son formalistas,
> hay que entenderlos--dijo Emilio
> Arévalo--. Están felices con el
> General y sólo piden que se guarden
> las formas democráticas. Odría
> electo y nos abrirán los brazos y
> nos darán los créditos que hagan
> falta. (I, p. 148)

The electoral process reveals three basic levels
of activity. First, there is the scheming and
manipulation of politicians such as Bermúdez, Espina,
and other high officials in the government. They
usually work in conjunction with members of the
oligarchy like Fermín Zavala. Secondly, there is the
behind the scenes activity of controlling the masses,
by force, as exemplified in Lozano's operation with

118

Hipólito and Ludovico. Third, there are the campaigns
of lesser politicians like Arévalo who utilizes
bodyguards such as Téllez, Urondo and Trifulcio to
literally steal elections. In the novelistic structure
of Conversación en La Catedral the different levels
of action are normally narrated in conjunction with
each other. As the author attempts to recreate the
complexities of the various experiences involved in
the political process, he suggests, by the fusing of
times, a never ending chain of events.

Cayo Bermúdez, a cholo, reluctantly accepts his
post as Director but once he experiences power realizes
that his potential is unlimited. Suffering basically
from an inferiority complex, he sets about to make
himself equal through ruthlessness and political
insight into the weaknesses of others. Being a sexual
pervert himself, he is quick to capitalize on the
latent homosexuality of Fermín Zavala, using Ambrosio
as the instrument. Queta and Hortensia are also used
to satisfy his voyeuristic needs while they satiate
their own homosexual impulses. Through the manipu-
lations of Cayo we explore the intimate relationships
of most elements of society.

Cayo develops into one of the most accomplished
politicians of his times. As one of the focal points
of the novel, he has contact with every major character
either directly or indirectly. However, in the manipulation of power he exceeds his limits. The threat
of revolution in Arequipa against the Administration,
which is historically documentable, and demands from
the Coalition force Cayo into exile.[25]

Cayo Bermúdez represents the baser aspects of
the Odría regime. From his portrayal, we can draw
many insights concerning the self serving interests
of power. The coarse language which he uses, his
perverted relationships, and his knowledge of the
weaknesses of others exemplify aspects of how a
dictator remains in control through fear and
manipulation.

Vargas Llosa recreates the Arequipa revolt from
multiple points of view in addition to particapants'
reactions. Señora Lucía receives her information
via the radio:

> . . . todas las actividades se habían
> paralizado en Arequipa, había habido

una manifestación en la Plaza de Armas
y los líderes de la Coalición habían
pedido nuevamente la renuncia del
Ministro de Gobierno, señor Cayo Bermúdez,
al que responsabilizaban por los graves
incidentes de la víspera en el Teatro
Municipal, el gobierno no había hecho
un llamado a la calma y advertido que
no toleraría desordenes. (I, pp. 326-27)

By utilizing intermediaries the author is able to
maintain an objective posture in the presentation of
the incident. Thus various reactions are presented
to give different perspectives to the event itself.
Cayo's end is signaled by the very forces which he
tried so hard to control:

> --Tienen el mayor respeto, por el
> Ejército, y sobre todo por usted,
> general Llerna--insistió el senador
> Landa--. Sólo piden que renuncie Ber-
> múdez. No es la primera vez que
> Bermúdez mete la pata, General, usted
> lo sabe. Es una buena ocasión para
> librar al régimen de un individuo que
> nos está perjudicando a todos, General.
> --Arequipa está indignada con lo
> del Municipal--dijo el general Alvarado--.
> Fue un error de cálculo del señor
> Bermúdez, mi General. Los líderes de
> la Coalición han orientado muy bien la
> indignación. Le echan toda la culpa
> a Bermúdez, no al régimen. Si usted
> me lo ordena, yo saco la tropa. Pero
> piénselo, mi General. Si Bermúdez
> sale del ministro, esto se resuelve
> pacíficamente.[26]

Cayo Bermúdez, the great manipulator, now finds
himself in the position of being forced out of the
government because he has incurred the wrath, not
only of the entire country but of his cohorts as well.
Incidents concerning Arequipa are conveyed to us both
secondhandedly, with reactions, and by direct participation in the events themselves as evidenced by
Trifulcio and Ludovico. Through various technical
devices, Vargas Llosa helps us to relive the hours
of demonstrations and maneuvering behind the scenes
which prompted this important historical event.

Cayo Bermúdez as representative of the regime exemplifies a syndrome which pervaded the Peruvian government during this era. Unable to gain the confidence of the people and govern, they resorted to various methods of control over their constituents which eventually lead to disaster.

Whenever Vargas Llosa deals with Peruvian history and politics the theme of APRA is usually present. In Conversación en La Catedral he is primarily concerned with aspects of the rhetorical phases of APRA and the persecution experienced by the party. As presented in the novel, APRA is more of an annoyance than an important political force--with much rhetoric and no constructive action.

The case of Trinidad López, who identifies with APRA, is exemplary of the type of political oppression which was dealt out after Odría came to power. Julio Cotler writes:

> Siguieron ocho años de brutal opresión: líderes sindicales apristas fueron asesinados, estudiantes encarcelados y nuevamente miles de militantes apristas se exiliaron. El Apra volvía, después de tres años de experiencia legal, a la vida de las "catacumbas" que había llevado durante 15 años.[27]

According to political scientists this persecution which the APRA experienced during the Odría period had profound effects on the party as a whole. Apparently it was during this period that APRA ceased to be a viable political force.

This period of political activity is extremely important in Peruvian history. The different fights, compromises and agreements among the parties which have taken place recently are reflected in the chaotic events in the novel. Although, superficially, the various political organizations were supposed to represent something different, the reality displayed in Conversación en La Catedral attests to the fact that there was much coexistence, be it peaceful or otherwise. This is exemplified in the elections of 1956 as Amalia tells Hortensia: "Ganó Prado, señora,

el Apra se le volteó a Lavalle y votó por Prado y
Prado ganó, así lo dijo la radio" (II, p. 101).

The complexity of the political situation is also
reflected in the observation which Santiago makes
concerning his father's burial:

> Había muchísima gente, sí Ambrosio
> hasta un edecán de la Presidencia,
> y al entrar al cementerio había
> llevado la cinta un momento un
> ministro pradista, un senador
> odriísta, un dirigente aprista y
> otro belaúndista. (II, p. 279)

As the different parties come and go we are treated to
a spectacle of political intrigue and dealings of the
intrahistoria of Peru, such as the populist rhetoric,
the buying and selling, and the underhanded maneuvering
to conceal the real truth. The repetition of certain
events and the reappearance of certain characters leave
the impression that history will probably repeat itself.

It is, indeed, in Conversación en La Catedral
that we see Vargas Llosa's most coherent view of
Peruvian history. History is being analyzed in terms
of political and social causality and developed in the
novel. The pattern of change is repetitious but we
witness the forces which function to maintain structures
and restrict individual movement. In contrast with
La casa verde, Conversación en La Catedral projects a
view of man as maker of history not as merely existing
in history. This is clearly exemplified by the figure
of Cayo Bermúdez who is determined to change not only
the course of events but also the very structure
of institutions.

Although there are dates and historical facts
throughout Conversación en La Catedral, Vargas Llosa
is not attempting to give us an objective account of
Peruvian history or of the function of APRA as a
historian might. Rather his narrative technique,
stressing the subjective accounts and memories of
Ambrosio and Santiago, functions to keep the work
focused on these literary characters and the
complexitites of their experiences. Needless to say,
this experience is bound up with history.

The conversation is expressive, in an intensely
personal manner of their inner convictions, beliefs,

dreams and ideals. This subjective mode of narration is opposed to the objective method which is basically impersonal, concerned principally with narrative, analysis, and external description--qualitites which are generally equated with historical method.

Selection, significance and shaping of material are important in the novelistic process of Conversación en La Catedral. Vargas Llosa as artist alters the historical material in the novel and yet maintains validity in presenting the beliefs, attitudes, and assumptions of society, which are in accordance with what is known of the mental and emotional climate of this period of Peruvian history. We are able to discern a great deal concerning quality of the inner life, the morality, heroism, and capacity for sacrifice peculiar to the age of Odría. The reader not only receives notions concerning Peruvian history and politics, but throughout shares the experiences of characters; their joy, guilt, defeat, and their final destinies. From top to bottom of society people are caught up in a tide of self interest in which everybody is affected by a legislated lack of morality.

The absence of declamatory rhetoric by the author is supplanted by believable situations, conversations, and actions by the characters themselves which are problematic. These are all presented in an expert implicit manner via style and technique. Themes are developed logically in conjunction with characters and plot thereby maintaining a coherent balance in the narrative.

The ochenio of Odría as interpreted by Vargas Llosa in Conversación en La Catedral was an era of corruption and betrayal of an entire nation of people. Elections were stolen, murder and torture committed, and individuals were forced to compromise their values in order to survive. His fictional characters give expression to the impact with which the historical events and personages had upon individuals living during this epoch.

Peruvian themes such as ethnicity, geography and urbanization are in evidence in the author's view of history. The class conflict between Fermín and Cayo, representing criollo and cholo respectively, is only part of the larger ethnic problem. Attitudes germinating in La ciudad y los perros are manifested

in a mature manner in <u>Conversación en La Catedral</u>. The
entire <u>criollo</u> segment of Peruvian society shows a
disdain for other strata. Odría, a mobile <u>cholo</u> who
had to rely heavily upon these people is not spared.
The Arévalo family makes its position of loyalty
quite clear in contrasting the weakness of Bustamante
with those of Odría:

> --Sería un calzonazos, pero era una
> persona decente y había sido diplomático
> --dijo la vieja de Popeye--. Odría, en
> cambio, es un soldadote y un cholo.
> --No te olvides que soy senador odríis-
> ta--se rió el senador--. Así que déjate
> de cholear a Odría, tontita. (I, p. 35)

Throughout the novels a degree of cynicism of this
nature pervades ethnic relations.

Geographically speaking, the tension between
urban and rural, developed and underdeveloped, coast
and <u>serranía</u>, remains one of the constants in the
conflicts between various factions. The plight of the
coastal Black lends ample testimony to this fact. The
cultural juxtaposition, whereby diversity and lack of
conformity result in different levels of human
development, lies at the heart of the imperfect ethnic
fusion in Vargas Llosa's novels. The process of
urbanization is a disheartening one in which individuals
are systematically punished in the attempt to become
acclimated. Amalia and Ambrosio are only a few of the
major characters who suffer greatly while trying to
survive. Urbanization as related to dehumanization
also weighs heavily upon Santiago.

LA CIUDAD Y LOS PERROS and PANTALEON Y LAS VISITADORAS

Prevalent also in Vargas Llosa's novels is the
Peruvian military which plays a significant role in the
outcome of individual destinies. As presented, the
military feels that its task is to impose order and
discipline upon individuals and upon institutions.
Victims of these attitudes range from upstart soldiers
who try to redefine the order of things, to civilians
who need to be made aware of realities of the country.
Among the most idealistic of Vargas Llosa's protagonists,
one finds a conflict between what was taught in
military school and the actual situation of the army.

In his book 100 Años del ejército peruano:
frustraciones y cambios,[28] Víctor Villanueva gives
a socio-psychological interpretation of the Peruvian
military structure. While offering an evaluation of
the present day situation of the army, Villanueva is
convinced that past action weighs heavily upon the
military mentality. Losses, especially to Chile and
Colombia, have instilled an inferiority complex which
the army has been unable to compensate for psychologically. One of Villanueva's main contentions is
that the army's basic ideology is transferred from one
generation to the next. Therefore instilled attitudes
remain alive through the ages and reflect built-in
military values and methods of compensation.

These theories ring remarkably true when applied
to Vargas Llosa's military protagonists. Gamboa and
Pantaleón exemplify this tendency to over react as
throughout the novels they not only relate their
functions to the social but also to the historical
military position of Peru. In the case of Gamboa, this
is quite evident in one of his assessments of the
country while observing the cadets with his superior:

> --Si algún día tuvieran que pelear
> de veras--dijo el capitán--, estos
> serían desertores o cobardes. Pero,
> por suerte para ellos, acá los milita-
> res sólo disparamos en las maniobras.
> No creo que el Perú tenga nunca una
> verdadera guerra.
> --Pero, mi capitán--repuso Gamboa--.
> Estamos rodeados de enemigos. Usted
> sabe que el Ecuador y Colombia esperan
> el momento oportuno para quitarnos un
> pedazo de selva. A Chile todavía no
> le hemos cobrado lo de Arica y Tarapaca.
> --Puro cuento--dijo el capitán,
> con un gesto escéptico--. Ahora todo
> lo arreglan los grandes. El 41 yo
> estuve en la campaña contra el Ecuador.
> Hubiéramos llegado hasta Quito. Pero
> se metieron los grandes y encontraron
> una solución diplomática, que tales
> riñones. Los civiles terminan resol-
> viendo todo. En el Perú, uno es
> militar por las puras huevas del diablo.
> --Antes era distinto--dijo Gamboa.[29]

The captain is taking the more cynical approach to the situation, realizing that cadets are not equipped to fight a war and that "los grandes" usually settle conflicts, not the soldiers themselves. Gamboa, on the other hand, believing the propaganda of military training is calling upon national history to justify his attitudes and actions. When he mentions "A Chile todavía no le hemos cobrado lo de Arica y Tarapaca," the 1879-1883 War of the Pacific in which Peru was thoroughly thrashed by Chile is alluded to. Unfortunately Gamboa only has negative consequences to call upon.

More significant however is the fact that a certain amount of tension between politicians and the military is being brought to light. This tension is also one of the driving forces behind relationships in Conversación en La Catedral. As perceived by the Captain in the above quote, the campaign into Ecuador which was ultimately stopped by politicians is apparently a common reaction by civilians which throughout history has become typical in their interference with the military.

In his assessment of political intervention in the war with Chile, Villanueva observes:

> Fue, principalmente, su lucha interna, personal, sectaria, falta de principios y de ética. Celos políticos parece que fueron la razón de que no se auxiliara a las tropas peruanas en la campaña del sur después de San Francisco, lo que no está debidamente probado y, lo que es peor, ni siquiera probado es que dichas tropas carecían casi de armamento, emprendieron su retirada hambrientos y semidesnudos.[30]

Wars undoubtedly have resulted in many frustrating campaigns for the Peruvian military. In La ciudad y los perros Gamboa appears to be suffering from a frustrated paranoia regarding the enemies of his country. Attitudes such as his have been engrained in the military mind during years of negative results. Vargas Llosa as interpreter of aspects of the military mentality shows an awareness of these attitudes in the portrayal of his characters.

Although his business is of a different nature
than Gamboa's, this awareness is foremost from the
beginning in the character of Pantaleón. This is evident in his response to Pochita's question"¿Leticia
es la parte colombiana de la selva, no?": "--Ahora es
Colombia, antes era Perú, nos la quitaron--. . . ."31
Both show, too, an obsession with getting the job
done at all costs without regard for the consequences.
Needless to say, Gamboa and Pantaleón end as frustrated exiles. This is part of a tendency, isolated by
Villanueva, to overcompensate for deficiencies experienced in the past. "La sobrevaloración, enteramente
subjetiva, que hace el militar de su institución, no
es, pues otra cosa que un mecanismo de defensa encam-
inado a cicatrizar las lesiones síquicas sufridas,"32
In the desire to protect the institution of the military, both Gamboa and Pantaleón compromise themselves.

In La ciudad y los perros Peruvian military history is imposed upon the students in crucial situations. For example, when Arana lies in state, the
narrator, a type of collective consciousness for the
cadets, is able to vicariously construct events:

> Y adivinaban también los ejemplos y
> las moralejas que exponía, el desfile
> de los próceres epónimos, de lso mártires
> de la Independencia y la Guerra con
> Chile, los héroes inmarcesibles que
> habían derramado su sangre generosa
> por la Patria en peligro. (p. 224)

During the eulogy of Arana, officials use tradition
to make it appear as if he were another patriotic sacrifice. They accomplish their ends by calling upon
the 'heroic' legacy of the military and relating it,
ironically, to el Esclavo's death--thereby pacifying
all elements involved.

While the young officers are infused with the urge
to succeed, the law and order forces of the military
are always in the background. The contradiction shown
in Gamboa and Pantaleón is that they are educated to
be good military men in the "tradition" but find
themselves inhibited by the very structure of the in-
struction. Combined with the control that the military
is shown to exercise over civilian life--conditioning
in La ciudad y los perros, exploitation and harassment
in La casa verde and Conversación en La Catedral--it is
shown to be one ominous presence, willing to define
what is "right" for Peruvian society.

127

After observing the bitter and pessimistic manner in which the functions of the Peruvian political,
social, and historical forces are expressed in Vargas
Llosa's novels, one must wonder about the author's
own feelings about these processes. After all, his
art is part the creation of social phenomena, origi-
nating to some extent from his relationship with society. In the interview with Alberto García Marrder,
significant questions were posed to Vargas Llosa concerning his own ideology (term which embraces any sub-
jectively coherent set of political beliefs):

> --Si no recuerdo mal, otra frase
> suya del coloquio en París de 1967
> fue la "única solución para los países
> latinoamericanos era la revolución
> armada". ¿Vale aún esa frase?
> --No usé esa frase. Siempre he pen-
> sado que la única solución para Amér-
> ica Latina es una revolución--es decir,
> un cambio radical de estructuras que
> libere a nuestros países de la camisa
> de fuerza que tienen tendida sobre
> ellos el imperialismo y las oligar-
> quías--; pero nunca creí que hubiera
> un única método--la lucha armada--para
> alcanzar esa revolución en todos los
> países latinoamericanos.
> Yo pensaba que en muchos de ellos--y
> entre estos el Perú, mi país--ese obje-
> tivo sólo se podría alcanzar mediante una
> revolución armada, debido al monolitismo
> de sus estructuras, a la naturaleza de
> su clase dirigente, al carácter de
> sus fuerzas armadas. En lo que respecta
> al Perú, yo no puedo afirmar la misma
> cosa de manera tan tajante. Es un hecho
> que la Junta Militar de gobierno que
> tomó el poder en el Perú hace un año y
> pico ha iniciado un proceso de cambio muy
> importante, y que por lo menos dos
> de las medidas que ha adaptado--la
> nacionalización del petróleo y la reforma
> agraria--tienen un carácter verdadera-
> mente revolucionario. La mejor prueba
> de ello es el solapado boicot a que
> tiene sometido al Perú el imperialismo
> en estos momentos y la hostilidad
> cerrada contra el régimen de la oli-
> garquía.[33]

For Vargas Llosa Socialism seems to be the road to follow in Peru and by extension Latin America since problems are similar. He appears to be advocating a controlled version of military socialism in the Cuban vein instead of the more liberal implementation of Chile, which has since resulted in disaster. One of the important questions inherent in this attitude is, without military leadership how can socialism be successful in Latin America? Allende, a civilian, tried and failed primarily because of the Oligarchy, the CIA, the Military, plus the withdrawal of United States aid. Vargas Llosa recognizes the importance of these forces when he speaks of the texture of a "revolución": ". . . es decir, un cambio radical de estructuras que libere a nuestros países de la camisa de fuerza que tienen tendida sobre ellos el imperial-ismo y las oligarquías--." One aspect of the political reality of Peru, revealed convincingly in Conversación en La Catedral is the fact that leaders change but nev-er the structures. The "cambio radical de estructuras" has not come about in various coups, counter coups, and political maneuvering. The Velasco regime was a step in that direction but two regimes later Peruvian his-tory seems to be repeating itself.

The historical process is viewed by Vargas Llosa as a series of convulsive events which in the long run served to perpetuate the system. This is exemplified in the position of Popeye after he has survived sev-eral administrations. El Chispas tells Santiago: "A Popeye le van muy bien los negocios ahora con Belaúnde en la presidencia ya sabes." (II, pp. 295-96) Popeye is maintaining the family's position in the oligarchy just as his father before him. But more important the comment serves to point out the real lack of changes in structures from Bustamamante to Belaúnde. Indeed Vargas Llosa's 1973 novel written post-Velasco, shows no glimmer of changes to come. Pantaleón y las visitadoras may be more realistic and pessimistic than his Paris pronouncement.[34]

In the light of the central question posed in this chapter, literature and history, there are several con-clusions which may be drawn. By creating valid literary characters to attend to his business with literature and placing them within the historical context, the artist does render an interpretation of history. In order for the reader to respond, the writer has to be faithful to both literature and history since one counterbalances the other. As a responsible craftsman

129

he deepens his literary projection of characters and events.

Vargas Llosa, as author, employs historical themes and incidents in his artistic recreation of periods of Peruvian history. Regardless of subject matter the artist's hand is always in evidence. Literarily, Vargas Llosa reconstructs personages, series of events, and captures the spirit of various ages and, as evidenced in interviews, pays the debt of serious scholarship to the facts of the period being recreated.

[1] The ending of Conversación en La Catedral touches the beginning of the Belaúnde Administration (1963-1968).

[2] "Realismo sin límites," Indice, Año XXII, Núm. 224 (octubre 1967), 22.

[3] Ibid.

[4] Amado Alonso, Ensayo sobre la novela histórica (Buenos Aires: Instituto de Filología, 1942), p. 115.

[5] George McMurray who is representative writes, "A pesar de que la acción cubre un período de más o menos cuarenta años--aproximadamente de 1920 a 1960 --ciertos aspectos de la trama, los personajes y el estilo, amplían las dimensiones temporales y espaciales abarcando conceptos que trascienden los límites de la simple narración." "Interpretaciones artísticas e históricas de 'La casa verde'" in Homenaje a Mario Vargas Llosa, ed. Helmy F. Giacoman and José Miguel Oviedo (New York: Las Américas, 1972), p. 183.

[6] R. J. Owens, Peru (London: Oxford University Press, 1964), p. 53.

[7] Mario Vargas Llosa, La casa verde (11th ed.; Barcelona: Seix Barral, 1971), p. 60. Hereafter cited in text.

[8] "Madurez de Vargas Llosa," Mundo Nuevo, Núm. 3, (septiembre 1966), p. 67.

[9] Typical is Frederick Pike's view that it was not until subsequent elections following Sánchez Cerro's death that the fascist tone of the party was set: "With political fragmentation having already advanced to an alarming rate, still another candidate appeared upon the scene in the person of Luis N. Flores. The candidate of the Revolutionary Union, which after the death of Sánchez Cerro had begun to assume fascistic leanings, Flores hoped that some of the assassinated cholo President's mass popularity would pass to him."

The Modern History of Peru (Washington: Praeger,
1967), p. 274.

[10]Peter Klarén, La formación de las haciendas
azucareras y los orígenes del APRA (Lima: Moncloa
Campodónico, 1970), p. 162.

[11]In his assessment of the functions of APRA during
this period Francois Bourricaud writes: "The Trujillo
rising of July 1932 made it possible to present Apra
as an anti-military organization. Some members of the
party, mostly peons from the sugar-cane plantation at
Laredo, captured the prefecture and the town hall
and installed as prefect a relative of Victor Raul, who
was in prison at Lima at the time. The rioters occupied
the O'Donovan barracks, and when the troops loyal to
Sánchez Cerro's government recovered the city, they
found the mutilated bodies of several dozen officers.
This rising--likened by El Comercio to the Paris Com-
mune--was not the first or last mutiny in which Apra
was involved; the most recent took place in October
1948, when part of the fleet stationed at Callao rose
against President Bustamante y Rivero. From 1932 to
1945, the army carried on a merciless fight against
Apra: in 1945-8 it acquiesced in the first convivencia
experiment, but immediately after the elections of 1962
it deposed Manuel Prado, who had been governing with
Apra support since 1956. Even during the period of
Apra's legality the military remained distrustful."
Power and Society in Contemporary Peru (Washington:
Praeger, 1970), p. 167.

[12]Pedro Ugarteche, Sánchez Cerro, II (Lima: Editorial Universitaria, 1969), p. 181.

[13]Klarén, pp. 160-61. Commenting on Sánchez
Cerro's popular support Frederick B. Pike adds: "Even
in the 'solid Aprista North', however, Sánchez Cerro
was by no means without his partisans. The residents
of his native Piura and also those of Tumbes were in
their great majority committed to the lieutenant
coronel turned politician." (Pike, p. 250).

[14]José Miguel Oviedo, Mario Vargas Llosa: la invención de una realidad (Barcelona: Barral, 1970), p.
124.

[15]Exemplary of the disagreement concerning Sánchez

Cerro and Piura are the opinions expressed by Carlos
Miró Quesada Laos. "Miguel es uno de los nombres que
la familia Sánchez Cerro escoge para el recién nacido.
Allí (Piura) habría de ver la luz de la patria. Su
modesta casa se halla en el no menos modesto barrio
de Tacalá. Pobreza suma acompaña sus primeros años.
Su padre ejercerá funciones de notario." Sánchez
Cerro y su tiempo (Buenos Aires: El Ateneo, 1947),
p. 35. The opposite view is taken by Pedro Ugarteche:
"Nació en la casa de sus mayores, situada en la zona
más residencial de la ciudad y no en el popular barrio
de Tacalá como se ha dicho y así lo recuerda una her-
mosa placa de bronce colocada por el Consejo Provin-
cial de Piura en homenaje a su memoria." Sánchez
Cerro, I (Lima: Universitaria, 1969), p. 2.

[16]Klarén, p. 162.

[17]Indice, p. 162.

[18]"The Peruvian Labyrinth," Times Literary Supplement, February 19, 1970, p. 208.

[19]Alberto J. Carlos interprets political implications of the work in "Conversación en La Catedral: novela política," Homenaje a Mario Vargas Llosa, pp. 407-
12.

[20]George Lukács, The Historical Novel, trans.
Hannah & Stanley Mitchell (London: Merlin Press, 1962),
p. 42. See also Helen Cam, Historical Novels (London:
Historical Association, 1961).

[21]"Vargas Llosa y el exilio del escritor latino-
americano," Indice, Año XXV, Núm. 263-64 (febrero 1970),
p. 28.

[22]César Lévano, "La novela de una frustración,"
Caretas, Núm. 420 (agosto 14-27 1970), p. 28.

[23]"Apacible fin de un exdictador," Oiga, Año XII,
Núm. 563 (22 de febrero de 1974), 18.

[24]Mario Vargas Llosa, Conversación en La Catedral,
2 vols. (5th ed.; Barcelona: Seix Barral, 1969), I,
p. 55. Cited hereafter in text.

[25]As seen by Carlos Miró Quesada Laos, this demonstration in Arequipa and the results represent one of the many ironies of this historical period: "Ahí pudo haber terminado el gobierno de Odría. Pero parece que los dirigentes de la Coalición fueron los primeros en ser tomados de sorpresa por la magnitud de la protesta y no estaban preparados para controlar los sucesos. Se limitaron a pedir por telegrama la destitución de Esparza. El gobierno de Odría estaba ya tan débil que el telegrama produjo inmediatas consecuencias y el repudiado Ministro tuvo que dejar la faja." Radiografía de la política peruana (2d ed.; Lima: Páginas Peruanas, 1959), p. 178.

[26]Conversación en La Catedral, II, p. 148.

[27]Julio Cotler, "Crisis política y populismo militar," Perú: Hoy (México: Siglo Veintiuno, 1971), p. 107.

[28]Victor Villanueva, 100 años del ejército peruano: frustraciones y cambios (Lima: Editorial Juan Mejía Baca, 1972).

[29]Mario Vargas Llosa, La ciudad y los perros (7th ed.; Barcelona: Seix Barral, 1971), p. 163.

[30]Villanueva, p. 43. This same opinion is expressed more encompassingly by Edgardo Mercado Jarrín who writes, "En la guerra de 1859 con el Ecuador, en 1866 con España, en 1879 con Chile y en el conflicto de 1941 con el Ecuador, las consideraciones políticas priman sobre la estrategia militar. La política conduce y dirige la guerra, poniendo en evidencia su supremacia." "La política nacional y la estrategia militar en el Perú," Oiga, Año XIII, Núm. 566 (abril 1970), pp. 13-55. See also Francois Bourricaud, "Los militares: ¿por qué y para qué?" Aportes, Núm. 16 (abril 1970), pp. 13-55.

[31]Mario Vargas Llosa, Pantaleón y las visitadoras (Barcelona: Seix Barral, 1974), p. 11.

[32]Villanueva, p. 89.

[33]Indice (febrero 1970), p. 43.

[34]For a thorough discussion of the military in
Vargas Llosa see Joseph Sommers, "Literature e ideo-
logía: el militarismo en las novelas de Vargas Llosa,"
Revista de Crítica Literaria Latinoamericana, Año 1,
No. 2 (1975), 87-112.

CHAPTER 5

LA TIA JULIA Y EL ESCRIBIDOR

AND A CONCLUSION

La tía Julia y el escribidor is considered, in part, a parody of the genre of the soap opera or radionovela/teatro which is one of the most important vehicles of popular culture consumption in Peru. Ramón Mendoza places the blame for their diffusion on the media barons in Latin America and alleges, "Soap operas have taken over the cultural world. They are modern 'opium of the people,' the most effective instrument of cultural and political alienation."[1]

There is no doubt that in many countries the mass media, through its promotion of escapist programming, is able to sublimate many serious aspects of daily life. If La tía Julia is a critical parody of the soap opera and middle class Peruvian values, it has been a success in reverse. The novel has the same function as the radioteatro. This is Vargas Llosa's most successful novel in terms of Peruvian readership because the audience sees itself and loves what it sees. In Peru, La tía Julia is not perceived by most people as a critical social statement.

However, La tía Julia y el escribidor, as non-problematic as it might seem, is a view of the opposite side of the Odría regime (1948-1956); the reverse of Conversación en La Catedral, Vargas Llosa's most caustic novel. La tía Julia is critical in the sense that a large majority of the population did not understand or did not care what was transpiring in Peru during the ochenio of Odría. Herein lies the novel's central irony. In fact, the narrator goes out of his way to remind the reader of La tía Julia's historical setting during Varguita's interview with a Mexican intellectual: ". . .porque el economista e historiador, en respuesta a una pregunta, atacó duramente a las dictaduras militares (en el Perú padecíamos una, encabezada por un tal Odría)."[2]

La tía Julia y el escribidor is, on the surface, less critical in nature in addressing the larger questions of society. It is, in part, autobiographical and does reflect many middle class Peruvian values and attitudes that were prevalent during the Odría era. Rather than upon "En qué momento se había jodido el Perú?", emphasis is placed on the author's love live and his perceptions of Pedro Camacho, the person who wrote soap operas. The sensational, the sentimental, and the improbable of the latter episodes, as well as the Peruvian presence in the autobiographical segments make the novel entertaining.

Popular culture and its diffusion is, of course, one of the major concerns of La tía Julia y el escribidor. Pedro Camacho, the Bolivian, is hired by Radio Central to produce radioteatros because it is too expensive to continue importing these programs from Cuba, of all places.3 They are classified as,

> . . . ese torrente de adulterios,
> suicidios, pasiones, encuentros,
> herencias, devociones, casualidades
> y crímenes que, desde la isla antilla-
> na, se esparcía por América Latina,
> para, cristalizado en las voces de
> los Lucianos Pandos y las Josefinas
> Sánchez, ilusionaron las tardes de
> las abuelas, las tías, las primas y
> los jubilados de cada país. (p. 14)

Corrupt, prerevolutionary Cuba is a fitting source for the dissemination of this escapist material throughout the Americas just as the post-revolutionary era has been the exporter of more socially enlightening commodities. Radio Panamericana, owned by the same persons but oriented toward a middle class audience in terms of programming, is the opposite of Radio Central whose mission is "multitudinaria, plebeya, criollísima." The description continues:

> Allí se propalaban pocas noticias y
> allí era reina y señora la música
> peruana, incluyendo a la andina, y
> no era infrecuente que los cantantes
> indios de los coliseos participaran
> en esas emisiones abiertas al público
> que congregaban muchedumbres, desde
> horas antes, a las puertas del local.
> (p. 12)

Much of the same social stratification endemic to Peruvian society is also evident in the attitude toward popular culture demonstrated by Panamericana and Central. While the former station concentrates upon world events, Hollywood gossip, and music from the U.S. top ten, the

latter is charged with filling a cultural void
experienced by people who migrate from the sierra and
the selva. Ironically, for the indígena who
participates in the coliseos, or folkloric exhibitions,
this is the first step toward becoming a consumer of
soaps. Within months the nostalgia for village life
wears off and the new arrivals begin to participate,
although marginally, in cosmopolitan limeñan society.
Acculturation is rapid and Pedro Camacho facilitates
this process through the production of material that
is acted out over the airwaves.

    Literary parody manifests itself in La tía Julia
y el escribidor beyond the surface imitation and
distortion of the radioteatro. First of all, at the
level of its escritura (that is, the novel considered
as a process or an act of writing), La tía Julia
combines two forms of discourse--the autobiographical
and the third person narrative--in alternating chapters
of plot development. But at both levels, the autobiographical and the novelistic, La tía Julia exhibits
and distorts the conventions to which it purports to
belong. Central to this distortion is the figure of
Pedro Camacho who is based upon the real life model of
Raúl Salmón. Their destinies do not coincide due to
poetic license. As creator of the third person soap
narrations, Camacho is a caricature in the autobiographical segments. Elements of fiction constantly
intrude elsewhere in the writer's fictional autobiography, thereby blurring the thin line between "real"
and "imagined" situations.

    Secondly, what becomes apparent early on in La tía
Julia y el escribidor is Vargas Llosa's parodic view of
the art of creative writing through the tripartite
dichotomies of escritor/escribidor, realidad/ficción,
and literatura/subliteratura. Pedro Camacho plays an
important role in these equations. From the moment he
appears on the scene, Camacho makes a lasting physical
and literary impression describing himself as, "Un ami-
go: Pedro Camacho, boliviano y artista" (p. 26). The
artistic dimension of Pedro Camacho is constantly
perplexing for Varguitas, the aspiring writer, who at
a crucial point in the narrative development reflects
upon his cohort:

            Qué medio social, qué encadenamiento
            de personas, relaciones, problemas,
            casualidades, hechos, habían producido

esa vocación literaria (¿literaria?
¿pero qué entonces?) que había
logrado realizarse, cristalizar en
una obra y obtener una audiencia?
¿Cómo se podía ser, de un lado, una
parodia de escritor y, al mismo
tiempo, el único que, por tiempo
consagrado a su oficio y obra reali-
zada, merecía ese nombre en el
Perú? (p. 235)

Within this ambiguous context the narrator raises a
question that is central to the thematic development
of La tía Julia y el escribidor: what is literature,
fiction in particular? In lines subsequent to the
above cited, the author questions the integrity of
part-time writers, politicians, pedagogs, lawyers
and others who have produced works but who do not live
only to write as does Pedro Camacho. In terms of a
pure writer, for Varguitas only Camacho is an
accessible model. This ironic conflict is stressed in
the above citation where Camacho is classified, "a
parody of a writer" who merits the label "scribbler."

In La tía Julia y el escribidor, Mario Vargas
Llosa, the novelist, is on the one hand writing the
story of Pedro Camacho while at the same time he is
penning his own romantic soap opera. The reader gets
a double dose of this "opium of the masses" through
the techniques of parody. Although La tía Julia y
el escribidor is written as an artist's autobiography
in a parodic mode, it also includes on a theoretical,
critical level a demonstration of the modern function
of parody. This is accomplished through the author's
manipulation of theme, structure, content and their
relationship to the overall meaning of the novel. For
Vargas Llosa parody in both creative imitation and
serious fun.

It is my view that in La tía Julia y el escribidor,
just as in Pantaleón y las visitadoras, the author
succeeds in juxtaposing the comic and the serious to
render a critical evaluation of Peruvian reality not
dissimilar to what was achieved in his earlier social
realist novels. Although irony and satire are elements
in all of Mario Vargas Llosa's novels, parody is
exploited to its fullest in La tía Julia y el
escribidor.

In this same vein, it is worthwhile to devote several paragraphs to La señorita de Tacna (1981), Vargas Llosa's only published dramatic work, which treats the disintegration of a Peruvian family. This erosion is presented from the perspectives of two opposites, Belisario, an aspiring writer, and Elvira, "La señorita de Tacna" who is a nonagenerian and the repository of family history. The two-act play is a projection of Belisario's imagination since he is in the act of creating a drama tinged with romanticism.

La señorita de Tacna is a work of contrasts, between youth and old age, history and fiction, truth and lie, dream and reality, past and present. The temporal and spatial poles are Tacna 1879-remote past, Lima 1950-past, and the world 1980-present. This drama incorporates, as do most of Vargas Llosa's works, veiled autobiographical references. Like La tía Julia y el escribidor, there are allusions to family situations and, among other things, to Pedro Camacho, creator of many radio soap operas.

Technically, there are numerous common places of Vargas Llosa's literary craft in La señorita de Tacna. In addition to different manifestations of montage in the narrative structure (cajas chinas, vasos comunicantes), Peru is the literary bedrock. As Belisario exorcises his demons, he realizes that he is feeding off the corpses of ancestors, drawing creative sustenance from the annals of family history, while, at the same time, keeping it alive through memory and the written and spoken word. These attitudes are standard in the literary theories of Mario Vargas Llosa.

Both La tía Julia y el escribidor and La señorita de Tacna in spite of being different in tone and style from the earlier novels, continue the critical culturalist trends in Vargas Llosa's fiction. This is not likely to change until Peru is able to determine its own political, social and economic destiny. That is, by imposing outside cultural standards, the country is denying itself an opportunity to progress.

This study has examined in detail four novels of Mario Vargas Llosa. Although my focus is essentially on content and meaning, ample attention has been devoted to technique. Themes common to La ciudad y los perros, La casa verde, Conversación en La Catedral, and Pantaleón y las visitadoras, such as heroism, irony, determinism, existentialism, and history were rigorously analyzed. In the novels discussed, cultural and

literary concerns are inextricably bound together
through innovative novelistic techniques. As a result,
the relationship between Peruvians themselves and with
the outside world is brought into focus. Vargas Llosa's
works are populated with characters from different
social strata; from the marginal Amazonian indígena
and the alienated urban Black to the most sophisticated
member of the limeñan aristocracy. They all share, to
varying degrees, the impact of the lie of underdevelopment upon Peru.

In general, the vision of reality portrayed is
pessimistic. Human beings are constantly at war with
themselves and their surroundings. This may be positive, however, in that it emphasizes the human capacity
for struggle and survival. Humans, it seems, have a
virtually unlimited capacity for suffering and sacrifice. In the four novels Vargas Llosa employs a modern conception of the heroic and emphasizes the ironic
nature of existence in his portrayal of characters.
These devices help to underscore individual destinies.

The Peruvian context reveals characters from all
walks of life engaged in social, political, psychological, and military conflicts. An air of ethnic nega-
tivity toward the lower classes pervades, which is
due both to the author's own class values as well as
to the reality of the country which Vargas Llosa is
fictionally portraying. Political groups, the oligarchy,
and the military are also criticized and blamed for
the lack of progress and for the solidification of
existing social and economic structures. Indeed, one
of Vargas Llosa's principal literary concerns is how
institutions impact upon individual destinies. These
attitudes are not likely to change since Peruvian history is often repetitive.

Vargas Llosa's command of narrative techniques,
especially point of view, structure, and time, has
enabled him to establish a coherent relationship
between form and content. This cohesion enhances the
formulation and expression of the author's unique vision of Peruvian reality. Technique, in conjunction
with character portrayal, reinforces situational presentation and underscores the human dramas enacted.

With La ciudad y los perros, La casa verde,
Conversación en La Catedral, and Pantaleón y las
visitadoras Mario Vargas Llosa has established himself
as one of Latin America's leading literary figures.
His conception of "literature is fire" emphasizes the

social dimension of these works. As an interpreter of the Peruvian experience, Vargas Llosa bridges the gap between fiction and reality while remaining faithful to his craft.

NOTES

[1]Ramón Mendoza, "A Slingshot at the Soap Giant,"
Caribbean Review, 8, No. 2 (1979), p. 48.

[2]Mario Vargas Llosa, *La tía Julia y el escribidor*
(Barcelona: Seix Barral, 1977), p. 272.

[3]The interpersonal basis of *La tía Julia y el
escribidor* is revealed in an article by Hubert Cam
entitled "Con La tía Julia." Julia comments positively
upon novelistic episodes of her marriage life and early
relationship with Mario. Apparently Raúl Salmón was
not satisfied with the manner in which he was characterized although he based his reaction on hearsay
evidence since he had not read the novel. According
to Cam, "En sucesivas conferencias de prensa, éste
(Salmón) amanezó al novelista con llevarlo a juicio.
Salmón, en Bolivia, es ahora el zar de la radio.
Editorializa 13 programas y posee la compañía emisora
más importante, Radio Nueva América, especializando en
noticieros y novelas. Ha publicado 33 comedias, un
libro en España y ya no escribe radioteatros." *Caretas*,
No. 529 (3 de nov. 1977), p. 56D.

MARIO VARGAS LLOSA:

SELECTED BIBLIOGRAPHY

Fictional Works by Vargas Llosa

Vargas Llosa, Mario. Los jefes. Barcelona: Rocas, 1959.

----------. La ciudad y los perros. Barcelona: Seix Barral, 1963.

----------. La casa verde. Barcelona: Seix Barral, 1966.

----------. Los cachorros: Pichula Cuéllar. Barcelona: Lumen, 1967.

----------. Conversación en La Catedral, 2 vols. Barcelona: Seix Barral, 1969.

----------. Pantaleón y las visitadoras. Barcelona: Seix Barral, 1969.

----------. La tía Julia y el escribidor. Barcelona: Seix Barral, 1977.

----------. La señorita de Tacna. Barcelona: Seix Barral, 1981.

----------. La guerra del fin del mundo. Barcelona: Seix Barral, 1981.

Critical Works by Vargas Llosa

Vargas Llosa, Mario. García Márquez: Historia de un deicidio. Barcelona: Barral, 1971.

----------.and Martín Riquer. El combate imaginario. Barcelona: Barral, 1972.

----------. La orgía perpetua: Flaubert y Madame Bovary. Barcelona: Seix Barral, 1975.

----------. José María Arguedas: Entre sapos y halcones. Madrid: Ediciones Cultura Hispánica, 1978.

----------. Entre Sartre y Camus. Río Piedras: Ediciones Huracán, 1981.

Major Studies on Vargas Llosa

Books

Boldori, Rosa. Mario Vargas Llosa y la literatura en el Perú de hoy. Santa Fe, Argentina: Colmegna, 1969.

Boldori de Baldussi, Rosa. Vargas Llosa: un narrador y sus demonios. Buenos Aires: Fernando García Cambeiro, 1974.

Cano Gaviria, Ricardo. El buitre y el ave fénix: Conversaciones con Vargas Llosa. Barcelona: Anagrama, 1972.

Díez, Luis Alfonso. Mario Vargas Llosa's Pursuit of the Total Novel. Cuernavaca, México: CIDOC, 1970.

Fenwick, M.J. Dependency Theory and Literary Analysis: Reflections on Vargas Llosa's The Green House. Minneapolis: Institute for the Study of Ideologies and Literature, 1981.

Fernández, Casto M. Aproximación formal a la novelística de Vargas Llosa. Madrid: Nacional, 1977.

Luchting, Wolfgang. Mario Vargas Llosa: Desarticulador de realidades: una introducción a sus obras. Bogotá: Plaza y Janes, 1978.

Martín, José Luis. La narrativa de Vargas Llosa: Acercamiento estilístico. Madrid: Gredos, 1974.

Oviedo, José Miguel. Mario Vargas Llosa: la invención de una realidad. Barcelona: Barral, 1970. 2nd ed., 1977.

Sommers, Joseph. Literature and Ideology: Vargas Llosa's Novelistic Evaluation of Militarism. Washington Square, N.Y.: NYU Occasional Papers, #15, 1975.

Critical Anthologies
These collections contain the best periodical articles devoted to Vargas Llosa.

Anon. Agresión a la realidad. Las Palmas, Islas Canarias: Letras a su Imán, 1972.

146

Diez, Luis A. Asedios a Vargas Llosa. Santiago de
     Chile: Universitaria, 1972.

Giacomán, Helmy F. Homenaje a Mario Vargas Llosa.
     Long Island City: Las Américas, 1972.

Homenaje a Vargas Llosa. Norte, año 12, no. 5-6 (1971).

Review (Spring 1975), Focus on Conversation in the
     Cathedral.

Rossman, Charles and Alan Friedman, eds. Texas Studies
     in Literature and Language, 19, no. 4 (1977).

Other Works Consulted

Alonso, Amado. Ensayo sobre la novela histórica.
     Buenos Aires: Instituto de Filología, 1972.

Amur, G.S. The Concept of Comedy. Dharwar, India:
     Karnatak University, 1963.

Anon. "Apacible fin de un exdictador," Oiga, No. 563
     (1974), 18-19.

----------. "La 'dimisión' de Bustamante," Oiga, No.
     511 (9 febrero 1973), 46-50.

Bejar, Hector. Peru 1965: Notes on Guerrilla
     Experience. New York: Monthly Review Press, 1970.

Berofsky, Bernard, ed. Free Will and Determinism.
     New York: Harper and Row, 1966.

Blackman, H.J., ed. Reality, Man and Existence:
     Essential Works of Existentialism. New York:
     Bantam Books, 1965.

Booth, Wayne C. The Rhetoric of Fiction. Chicago:
     University of Chicago Press, 1961.

----------. A Rhetoric of Irony. Chicago: University
     of Chicago Press, 1974.

Bourricaud, Francois. Power and Society in Contemporary
     Peru. trans. Paul Stevenson. New York: Praeger,
     1970.

Braudy, Leo. Narrative Form in History and Fiction.
     Princeton: Princeton University Press, 1970.

Brombert, Victor, ed. The Hero in Literature. New
York: Fawcett, 1969.

Brotherston, Gordon. The Emergence of the Latin American Novel. New York: Cambridge University
Press, 1977.

Brown, J. A. C. Freud and the Post-Freudians. Baltimore: Penguin Books, 1966.

Brushwood, John. "Latin-American Literature and History: Experience and Interpretation," Hispania,
Vol. 54, No. 1 (March 1971), 89-99.

Cam, Helen. Historical Novels. London: Historical
Association, 1961.

Campbell, Joseph. The Hero with a Thousand Faces.
New York: Meredian Books, 1956.

Campos, Julieta. Función de la novela. México:
Joaquín Mortiz, 1973.

Christensen, Nadia Margaret. "A Comparative Study of
the Anti-Hero in Danish and American Fiction,"
Unpublished Ph.D. dissertation, University of
Washington, 1972.

Clark, Gerald. "The Need for New Myths," Time, January
17, 1972, pp. 50-51.

Daiches, David. The Novel and the Modern World.
Chicago: University of Chicago Press, 1960.

Dellboy, Alfonso. "La ruta peruana," Indice, No. 353
(15 mayo 1974), 9-14.

Davis, Robert Murray, ed. The Novel: Modern Essays
in Criticism. Englewood Cliffs: Prentice Hall,
1969.

D'Angelo, Edward. The Problem of Freedom and Determinism. Columbia: University of Missouri Press,
1968.

Delgado, Carlos, ed. Problemas sociales en el Perú
contemporáneo. Lima: Moncloa Campodónico, 1971.

----------. El proceso revolucionario peruano: testimonio de lucha. México: Siglo Veintiuno, 1972.

----------., et. al. <u>Perú: Hoy</u>, 2d. ed. México:
    Sigo Veintiuno, 1971.

Dorfman, Ariel. <u>Imaginación y violencia en América</u>.
    Santiago de Chile: Universitaria, 1970.

Dworkin, Gerald, ed. <u>Determinism, Free Will and Moral</u>
    <u>Responsibility</u>. Englewood Cliffs: Prentice
    Hall, 1970.

Dyson, A. E. <u>The Crazy Fabric: Essays in Irony</u>. New
    York: St. Martin's Press, 1965.

Edwards, Paul, ed. <u>The Encyclopedia of Philsophy</u>, 26
    vols. New York: MacMillan, 1967.

Fleischer, Helmut. <u>Marxism and History</u>. trans. Eric
    Mosbacher. New York: Harper Torchbooks, 1973.

Forgues, Roland. "Lectura de <u>Los cachorros</u> de Mario
    Vargas Llosa," <u>Hispamérica</u>, Año V, No. 13
    (abril 1976), 33-49.

Fox, Lucía. <u>El rostro de la patria en la literatura</u>
    <u>peruana</u>. Buenos Aires: Continente, 1970.

Franco, Jean. <u>Introduction to Spanish American Liter-</u>
    <u>ature</u>. Cambridge: Cambridge University Press,
    1969.
----------. <u>Spanish American Literature Since Inde-</u>
    <u>pendence</u>. New York: Barnes and Noble, 1973.

Frank, Roslyn M. "El estilo de <u>Los cachorros</u>," <u>Anales</u>
    <u>de la Literaturea Hispanoamericana</u>, No. 2&3
    (1973-74), 569-91.

Franklin, R. L. <u>Freewill and Determinism</u>. New York:
    Humanities Press, 1958.

Fromm, Erich. <u>Man for Himself</u>. New York: Fawcett,
    1969.

Frye, Northrop. <u>The Critical Path</u>. Bloomington:
    Indiana University Press, 1971.

----------. <u>Anatomy of Criticism</u>. Princeton: Prince-
    ton University Press, 1957.

Fuentes, Carlos. <u>La nueva novela hispanoamericana</u>,
    3rd. ed. México: Joaquín Mortiz, 1972.

Gallagher, D. P. Modern Latin American Literature.
New York: Oxford Universtiy Press, 1973.

Ghiselin, Brewster, ed. The Creative Process. New
York: Mentor Books, 1952.

Giraud, Ramon. The Unheroic Hero in the Novels of
Stendhal, Balzac and Flaubert. New Brunswick:
Rutgers University Press, 1957.

Glicksberg, Charles I. The Ironic Vision in Modern
Literature. The Hague: Martinus Nijhoff, 1969.

Guerin, Wilfred L. et. al. A Handbook of Critical
Approaches to Literature. New York: Harper
and Row, 1966.

Hamilton, Carlos D. "La novela actual de Hispanoamér-
ica," Cuadernos Americanos, No. 2 (mar-abr 1973),
223-51.

Harss, Luis and Barbara Dohmann. Into the Mainstream.
New York: Harper and Row, 1967.

Hayden, Rose Lee. An Existential Focus on Some Novels
of the River Plate. East Lansing: Latin American
Studies Center, 1973.

Hazera, Lydia de León. La novela de la selva hispano-
americana. Bogotá: Caro y Cuervo, 1971.

Holman, C. Hugh, ed. A Handbook to Literature, 2d. ed.
New York: Odyssey Press, 1960.

Hook, Sidney, ed. Determinism and Freedom. New York:
New York University Press, 1958.

Howe, Irving. Politics and the Novel. New York:
Meredian press, 1958.

Humphrey, Robert. Stream of Consciousness in the
Modern Novel. Berkeley: University of California
Press, 1968.

Ismodes Cairo, Aníbal. Sociología del Perú. 2d. ed.
Lima: Rocarme, 1969.

Josephson, Eric and Mary, eds. Man Alone. New York:
Harvest Books, 1933.

Jung, C. G. Modern Man in Search of a Soul. New

York: Harvest Books, 1933.

Kierkegaard, Søren. The Concept of Irony. trans.
Lee M. Capel. New York: Harper and Row, 1965.

Klapp, Orrin E. Heroes, Villains, Fools. Englewood
Cliffs: Prentice Hall, 1962.

Klarén, Peter. La formación de las haciendas azucareras y los orígenes del APRA. Lima: Moncloa

Larson, Magali Sarfatti and Arlene Eisen Bergman.
Social Stratification in Perú. Berkeley: Institute of International Studies, 1969.

Laurenson, Diana and Alan Swingewood. The Sociology
of Literature. London: MacGibbon and Kee, 1971.

Lazo, Raimundo. La novela andina. México: Porrúa, 1971.

Levin, Harry. Contexts of Criticism. New York:
Antheneum, 1963.

Lindquist, Sven. The Shadow: Latin American Faces the
Seventies. Baltimore: Pelican Books, 1972.

Lowenthal, Leo. Literature, Popular Culture, and Society. Palo Alto: Pacific Books, 1961.

Luchting, Wolfgang A. Pasos a desnivel. Caracas:
Mote Avila, 1974.

Lukács, Georg. The Theory of the Novel, trans. Anna
Bostock. Cambridge: M.I.T. Press, 1961.

----------. The Historical Novel, trans. Hannah
and Stanley Mitchell. London: Merlin Press,
1962.

Macías de Cortaya, Graziella. "La novela hispanoamericana actual como exponente de las técnicas mod-
ernas," Horizontes, No. 26 (abril 1970), 5-32.

Marcus, Steven. "Historical Novels," Harper's, 248,
No. 1486 (March 1974), 85-90.

Mariátegui, José Carlos. Ideología y política, 2d. ed.
Lima: Amauta, 1971.

----------. Siete ensayos de interpretación de la realidad peruana, 19th ed. Lima: Amauta, 1971.

Marín Morales, José Alberto. "Siete novelistas his-
    pano-americanos," Arbor, No. 293 (mayo 1970),
    27-43.

Matilla Rivas, Alfredo. "Los jefes o las coordenadas
    de la escritura vargas llosiana," Nueva Narrativa
    Hispanoamericana, Vol. 1, No. 2 (1971), 57-63.

Matos Mar, José, et. al. El Perú actual. México:
    Universidad Nacional, 1970.

McElroy, Davis Dunbar. Existentialism and Modern Lit-
    erature, 3rd. ed. New York: Citadel Press, 1966.

Mendilow, A. A. Time and the Novel. 1952; rpt.
    New York: Humanities Press, 1972.

Mercado Jarrín, Edgardo. "Las leyes del Perú," Indice,
    No. 338-339 (1 y 15 de octubre de 1973), 21-23.

Milne, Gordon. The American Political Novel. Norman:
    University of Oklahoma Press, 1966.

Miró Quesada Laos, Carlos. Sánchez Cerro y su tiempo.
    Buenos Aires: El Ateneo, 1947.

----------. Radiografía de la política peruana,
    Lima: Páginas Peruanas, 1959.

Monroe, N. Elizabeth. The Novel and Society. Chapel
    Hill: University of North Carolina Press, 1941.

Muecke, D. C. Irony. London: Methuen, 1970.

----------. The Compass of Irony. London: Methuen,
    1970.

O'Faolain, Sean. The Vanishing Hero. London: Eyre
    and Spottiswode, 1956.

Olson, Elder. The Theory of Comedy. Bloomington:
    Indiana University Press, 1968.

Ortega, Julio. La imaginación crítica. Lima: Peisa,
    1975.

Oviedo, José Miguel. "Literatura peruana hoy," Casa
    de las Américas, No. 64 (enero-febrero 1971),
    21-27.

Owens, R. J. Peru. New York: Oxford University

Press, 1963.

Panorama actual de la literatura latinoamericana.
    Caracas: Fundamentos, 1971.

Pendle, George. A History of Latin America. Balti-
    more: Pelican Books, 1969.

Pike, Fredrick B. The Modern History of Peru. Wash-
    ington: Praeger, 1967.

Preminger, Alex, ed. Encyclopedia of Poetry and
    Poetics. Princeton: Princeton University Press,
    1965.

Rama, Angel. García Márquez y la problemática de la
    novela. Buenos Aires: Corregidor-Marcha, 1974.

Rama, Carlos M. La historia y la novela. Buenos
    Aires: Nova, 1970.

Sábato, Ernesto. "Sartre contra Sartre o la misión
    trascendente de la novela," Casa de las Américas,
    No. 47 (marzo-abril 1968), 30-41.

Salazar Bondy, Sebastián. Lima la horrible, 3d. ed.
    México: Era, 1968.

Sale, Roger. Modern Heroism. Berkeley: University of
    California Press, 1973.

Sartre, Jean Paul. Existentialism and Human Emotions,
    trans. Edith Barnes. Secaucus: Citadel Press,
    1957.

----------. What is Literature?, trans. Bernard
    Frechtman. New York: Harper and Row, 1965.

----------. Politics and Literature, trans. J. A.
    Underwood and John Calder. London: Calder and
    Boyars, 1973.

Scholes, Robert, ed. Approaches to the Novel. San
    Francisco: Chandler, 1966.

Scott, Wilber S., ed. Five Approaches of Literary
    Criticism. New York: Collier Books, 1962.

Sommers, Joseph. After the Storm. Albuquerque: Uni-
    versity of New Mexico Press, 1968.

Stern, Alfred. Sartre, 2d. ed. New York: Dell, 1967.

Suhl, Benjamin. Jean Paul Sartre: The Philosopher as a Literary Critic. New York: Columbia University Press, 1970.

Swabey, Marie Collins. Comic Laughter. New Haven: Yale University Press, 1961.

Sypher, Wylie, ed. Comedy. New York: Anchor Books, 1956.

Ugarteche, Pedro. Sánchez Cerro, 3 vols. Lima: Universitaria, 1969.

Vargas Llosa, Mario. García Márquez: Historia de un decidido. Barcelona: Barral, 1971.

Villanueva, Victor. ¿Nueva mentalidad militar en el Perú? Buenos Aires: Replantes, 1969.

----------. 100 años del ejército peruano. Lima: Juan Mejía Baca, 1972.

Villegas, Juan. La estructura mítica del héroe. Barcelona: Planeta, 1973.

Warnock, Mary, ed. Sartre. New York: Anchor Books, 1971.

Wellek, René. Concepts of Criticism. New Haven: Yale University Press, 1963.

---------- and Austin Warren. Theory of Literature, 3rd. ed. New York: Harvest Books, 1956.

Wisse, Ruth R. The Schlemiel as Modern Hero. Chicago: University of Chicago Press, 1971.

Wolf, Eric R. and Edward C. Hansen. The Human Condition in Latin America. New York: Oxford University Press, 1972.

Wright, Andrew H. "Irony and Fiction," The Journal of Aesthetics and Art Criticism, 12, No. 1 (1953), 111-18.

ABOUT THE AUTHOR

Marvin A. Lewis teaches Spanish American, Afro-Hispanic, and Hispanic minority literature at the University of Illinois-Urbana. His book on Afro-Hispanic poetry is forthcoming.